Little Hands Fingerplays & Action Songs

Seasonal Activities & Creative Play for 2- to 6-Year-Olds

Emily Stetson & Vicky Congdon

Illustrations by Betsy Day

Winner of the Parents' Choice Approved Award

WILLIAMSON PUBLISHING  CHARLOTTE, VERMONT

Library of Congress Cataloging-in-Publication Data

Stetson, Emily, 1957-
    Little Hands fingerplays & action songs : seasonal rhymes & creative play for 2- to 6-year-olds / Emily Stetson & Vicky Congdon.
        p. cm. — (A Williamson Little Hands book)
    Includes index.
    ISBN 1-885593-53-8 (pbk.)
    1. Finger play—Juvenile literature. 2. Rhyming games—Juvenile literature. [1. Finger play. 2. Nursery rhymes. 3. Games.] I. Title: Little hands fingerplays and action songs. II. Congdon, Vicky, 1958- III. Title. IV. Series.

GV1218.F5 S73 2001
793.4—dc21

2001017697

Little Hands® series editor: **Susan Williamson**
Interior design: **Nancy-jo Funaro**
Illustrations: **Betsy Day**
Cover design: **Trezzo-Braren Studio**
Printing: **Capital City Press**

Williamson Publishing Co.
P.O. Box 185
Charlotte, VT 05445
(800) 234-8791

Manufactured in the United States of America

10 9 8 7 6 5 4 3

Little Hands®, *Kids Can!*®, *Tales Alive!*®, and *Kaleidoscope Kids*® are registered trademarks of Williamson Publishing.

Good Times™, *Little Hands Story Corner*™, and *Quick Starts for Kids!*™ are trademarks of Williamson Publishing.

Dedication

To my mother, Edith Hurd Stetson, who taught me my first fingerplays and nursery rhymes, and to my daughters, Erin, Laura, and Annie, who carry on the tradition of sharing songs, stories, and silly rhymes.

—E.S.

For my daughters, Gina and Katy, who both share my love of language, song, and just plain silliness, and with thanks to my mom, Mary Eleanor Schenke, for the special memories of all the songs, rhymes, and stories we shared.

—V.C.

Permissions

Permission to use activities from the following Williamson Publishing authors is granted: Laurie Carlson, Nancy Castaldo, Laura Check, Jill Frankel Hauser, Mary Tomczyk, Judy Press, and Susan Williamson.

Acknowledgments

The fingerplays and action songs were provided by Sandra Gazo and Tiny Tots Preschool in Burlington, Vermont, except as noted below:
"Little Miss Ladybug," "Bug Countdown," "Bugs Are Neat!," and "Three Little Fireflies" from *Storytime Treasures* newsletter; "Five Little Birds," "Baby Birds," and "Snowflakes Falling" from the National Network for Child Care; "Dr. King, He Had a Dream" from <www.geocities.com>; "Independence Day" and "Kwanzaa Is Here!" from <perpetualpreschool.com>; "Inchworm, Inchworm," "Here Come the Ducks," "The Elephant," "Pitter Pat," and "My Kitty" from *Alphabet Art* by Judy Press; "I'm a Tall, Tall, Tree" ("This Is My Trunk") from *Yonder Come Day: Traditional Music for Children* by Mary DesRosiers and Friends.

CONTENTS

For a complete list of activities to go with each fingerplay, see pages 125–126.

LET'S GO!

Ready to sing and ready to wiggle?
And, of course, are you ready to giggle?
There's something special about these rhymes,
Because they get you moving at the same time!

Your favorites are here — and new ones, too,
And they all come with actions that you can do!
Do the motions yourself, or with a friend,
Can you both stretch all the way to the end?

Wave your "branches" like a tree,
Zoom your hand like a busy bee,
Shape your fingers like round owl eyes,
Now you're a sun that brightens the skies.

Be a brave firefighter, a high-flying kite,
Time to flap those "wings" with all your might!
A falling raindrop, a blossom in spring,
Did you know you could become so many things?

Shake, and jump, and keep the beat,
Clap your hands and stomp your feet,
With some of these verses,
anything goes,
As you have
fun from your
head to your toes!

TO THE GROWN-UPS

Welcome to the world of fingerplays and action songs! Kids love these easy-to-learn rhymes and songs that let them stretch their active imaginations and their bodies from head to toe. While they're stomping out the beat, hopping like bunnies, or waving their "branches" in the wind, they're developing their verbal, musical, rhythm, and motor skills — without realizing it!

No wonder kids respond so enthusiastically to these rhymes. Fingerplays and action songs are a natural extension of children's love of pretend play. Whether it's a busy bee or a brave firefighter, they are ready to play the part. We have suggested motions for each line, but be sure to leave plenty of room for improvisation. Add a simple prop like a gauzy scarf for wings, and watch the creativity blossom!

The seasonal format allows kids to explore their world through the familiar themes they love — holidays, families, nature, animals, and the changing weather. Easy crafts and favorite stories are suggested to expand the learning and add to the fun, creating brief thematic interludes that give meaning to the changing seasons.

But there's more going on here than meets the eye. The seemingly simple act of dramatizing a song or rhyme reinforces critical pre- and early reading skills. Through repetition of the words, kids absorb the rhythm and flow of our language. Adding motions helps them to translate what they are hearing into mental images, developing memory skills and reinforcing the meaning of the words. In this interactive way, kids build a reading vocabulary as well as learn concepts like numbers, shapes, and directions (up, down, right, left).

Fingerplays and action songs are ideal for practicing social skills, too. Active kids slow down and "tune in," while still enjoying a creative outlet for their energy. Quieter children blossom as they eagerly match words with motions. Performed as a group, these songs help kids develop sharing skills as they alternate parts and take turns.

Best of all, fingerplays and action songs are fun and memorable. As we compiled this collection, we recalled special moments shared with our mothers, as well as snuggles and giggles with our own kids. We offer this collection to you, and the children in your lives, so you can appreciate the richness of these simple childhood songs and verses, and pass them on to the next generation of wigglers and gigglers.

THREE CHEERS FOR FALL!

The apples and pumpkins are ripe for picking, leaves are changing colors, the weather's turning chillier, kids are going to school — it's fall! Join in the fun of the season with your fingers, voice, and whole body as you gather the harvest, jump in the leaves, fly like a migrating bird, make new friends, pretend to be a wide-eyed owl, and celebrate being together!

Bring in the Harvest!

Apples, carrots, and pumpkins galore — pick them all! What are the colors and shapes of the fall harvest? Using songs and motions, dig beneath green tops for orange carrots, reach way up in a tree for apples ripe and red, and choose a round, orange pumpkin from the pumpkin patch!

Pumpkin, Pumpkin

To the tune of "Twinkle, Twinkle Little Star."

Pumpkin, pumpkin on the ground,
> *(crouch down)*

How'd you get so big and round?
> *(stretch arms out to sides, then into a big circle)*

Once you were a seed so small,
> *(pretend to hold a tiny seed between two fingers)*

Now you are a great big ball!
> *(form arms into a big circle)*

Pumpkin, pumpkin on the ground,
> *(crouch down)*

How'd you get so big and round?
> *(stretch arms out to sides, then into a big circle)*

Pulling Up Carrots

Think of all your favorite vegetables and fruits, and decide which ones you "pick," which you "pull," and which you "dig." Add verses to include them all!

To the tune of "Way Down Yonder in the Paw-Paw Patch," repeating the motion throughout the verse.

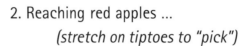

Pulling up carrots, put them in your basket,
> *(bend down to "harvest carrots,"*
> *then place in "basket")*

Pulling up carrots, put them in your basket,

Pulling up carrots, put them in your basket,

Way down yonder in the carrot patch!
> *(point far away)*

2. Reaching red apples ...
> *(stretch on tiptoes to "pick")*

3. Digging some potatoes ...
> *(dig in "dirt")*

4. Picking tiny berries ...
> *(gently pick with fingers)*

Make a Popsicle-stick carrot patch!

What you need: green construction paper (cut in half), child safety scissors, glue, craft or Popsicle sticks, orange marker, cotton balls

- CUT OUT CARROT TOPS; GLUE TO STICKS
- COLOR STICKS
- CUT SLITS; INSERT "CARROTS"
- DRAW BUNNY
- GLUE ON COTTON-BALL TAIL

The Carrot Song

Here's a harvest song you can sing with a group or by yourself! Use one name or "build names"* as you go.

To the tune of "Over in the Meadow."

Out in the garden under the sun,
> *(form circle around head with arms)*

Grew some carrots, and <u>(child's name)</u> picked one,
> *(child named bends over and "picks")*

Out in the garden under skies so blue,
> *(hands up in the air)*

Grew some carrots, <u>(child's name)</u> picked two,
> *(child named bends over and picks)*

Out in the garden near a big oak tree,
> *(make a "tree" with body and arms)*

Grew some carrots, <u>(child's name)</u> picked three,
> *(child named bends over and picks)*

We took those carrots, and we washed the whole bunch,
> *("washing" actions)*

Then we sat right down,
> *(sit on floor)*

and we ate them all for lunch,
> *(munching motions)*

"Munch, munch, munch, munch, munch!"

**"Building names" means you repeat all the names, adding on a new one each time (Laura, then Laura and Annie, then Laura, Annie, and Tyler).*

✓ Check the Calendar

World Food Day

With so much food to harvest, it's hard to imagine not having enough to eat! But there are people going hungry all over the world — even where you live! World Food Day in October is a special time to give a helping hand to others who may be hungry.

The next time you're at the grocery store, ask a grown-up in your family to buy an extra box of your favorite pasta or some other canned or boxed foods. Then, together, deliver them to your local food shelf. Thanks for doing your part to help stop hunger!

Little Hands Story Corner™

Flying Carrots
> by S.A. Cornell

Growing Vegetable Soup
> by Lois Ehlert

Apples and Pumpkins
> by Anne F. Rockwell

Too Many Pumpkins
> by Linda White

Apple Tree

Here is a tree with leaves so green,

(make a "tree" with arms and body)

Here are the apples that hang in between,

(form circle with hands)

When the wind blows,

(sway body and wave arms together over head)

The apples will fall,

(bring arms and fingers down and crouch down)

Here is the basket to gather them all!

(form "basket" with arms)

Make apple star prints

There's a surprise inside every apple! Can you find it?

What you need: apple, knife (for grown-up use), red tempera paint, construction paper, glue

- DIP CUT APPLE IN PAINT
- PRINT ON PAPER
- GLUE SEEDS IN CENTER "STAR"

Five Ripe Apples

Five ripe apples up in a tree,

> *(hold five fingers up; make a "tree" with body and arms)*

One looked down and smiled at me,

> *(look down and smile)*

So I twisted that apple as hard as I could,

> *(stretch arm up high and twist hand)*

Yum! Yum! It was good!

> *("bite" apple and rub tummy)*

Repeat verses and motions, counting down on your fingers:

2. Four ripe apples ...
3. Three ripe apples ...
4. Two ripe apples ...

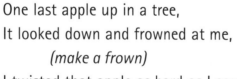

Last verse:

One last apple up in a tree,

It looked down and frowned at me,

> *(make a frown)*

I twisted that apple as hard as I could,

> *(stretch arm up high and twist hand)*

Eeww! It was rotten!

> *(grimace at the "rotten apple" in hand)*

Peel an Apple

Act out these motions and see what you get!

Peel an apple,

Cut it up,

And cook it in a pot!

When you eat it,

You will find,

It's applesauce you've got!

Make homemade applesauce

What you need: apples, saucepan, water, potato masher or fork

Rinse about eight apples and ask a grown-up to peel, core, and cut them into chunks. Place the chunks in a saucepan with $1^1/_2$ cups (375 ml) water. Cover the pan and simmer the apples until they are soft. Let cool and mash. Then serve yourself a bowl of sweet applesauce (try it over vanilla ice cream for an extra-special treat!).

Cinnamon-sugar applesauce:
Add $^1/_8$ cup (25 ml) sugar and 1 teaspoon (5 ml) of cinnamon.

Check the Calendar

Johnny Appleseed

Johnny Appleseed was the nickname given to John Chapman, who lived more than 200 years ago. As the story goes, John walked across the land, carrying apple seeds in a sack and planting them everywhere he went. Those little seeds grew into great big apple trees! John Chapman's birthday is on September 26 — right in the middle of apple-harvesting season. Celebrate his birthday by going apple picking!

Little Hands Story Corner™

Rain Makes Applesauce
    by Julian Scheer
The Seasons of Arnold's Apple Tree
    by Gail Gibbons
The Story of Johnny Appleseed
    by Aliki
Johnny Appleseed
    by Steven Kellogg

The Leaves Are Falling!

Get ready — the show is about to begin! Mother Nature puts on a glorious display in the fall, as the leaves turn brilliant colors. You can put on a show of the changing season, too, using your fingers and voice as falling leaves, swaying your whole body like the fall wind, and playing fall charades! Fall is so much fun!

Ten Bright Leaves

Ten little leaves up in a tree,
> *(hold up all 10 fingers)*

They're as bright as they can be,

Along comes the wind blowing all around,
> *(wave fingers in the air)*

And one bright leaf falls to the ground.
> *(flutter hand and fold down one finger)*

Repeat the verse, counting down on fingers to one:

2. Nine little leaves ...
3. Eight little leaves ...

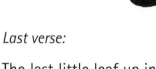

Last verse:

The last little leaf up in a tree,
> *(one finger up)*

It's as bright as it can be,

Along comes the wind blowing all around,
> *(wave last finger)*

And the last little leaf falls to the ground.
> *(fold down finger and crouch down)*

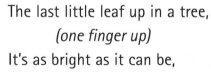

Fall Winds

Fall winds begin to blow,
(make your body sway)
Colored leaves fall fast and slow,
(flutter fingers to ground)
Twirling, whirling all around,
(turn self around, arms out at sides)
Till at last, they touch the ground.
(let hands fall to ground)

Sort leaves

Go on a nature walk outside with a grown-up and gather some leaves. Sort them by color and then by size.
What other ways can you sort them?

Falling Leaves

Start on tiptoes and slowly move down to the floor, just like a leaf falling gracefully through the air!

Down,
        down,
Yellow
        and
                brown,
Leaves
        are
                falling,
Over
        the
                town!

Check the Calendar

The first day of autumn

The signs of fall are different everywhere. How do you know it's autumn where you live? Think about the foods being harvested in gardens or what the trees and bushes look like. Has the air gotten so chilly that you need to wear a jacket? Have any leaves begun to turn color?

Around September 20, in the Northern Hemisphere, summer officially ends and autumn begins every year. But in some northern areas, it may feel like fall long before then, as the days grow shorter, the nights become longer, and the weather gets colder. In other places, it may feel like summer almost all year long!

Leaf Pile

When the leaves are on the ground,
  (flutter hands to the floor)
Instead of on the trees,
  *(arms outstretched and fingers
  stretched like branches)*
I like to make a great big pile,
  (arch hands over "leaf pile")
Way up to my knees,
  (hands on knees)
Then I run and jump in them,
  (jump up and down)
As silly as you please!
  (act out silly motions)

Play fall charades!

Can your friends guess what you are doing as you act out these fall activities? Don't forget: No words — just motions!

- Squirrels gathering nuts
- Leaves floating to the ground
- Raking leaves
- Birds flying south
- Putting on jackets
- Gathering vegetables
- Animals hibernating

Little Hands Story Corner™

Now It's Fall
  by Lois Lenski
When Autumn Comes
  by Robert Maass

Animal Friends

Your animal friends are busy in the fall, getting ready for winter! Some are gathering nuts, others are flying south to warmer homes, and some are eating all they can to store up fat for a long winter's nap. Act like a squirrel, count out nuts (and go on a squirrel-style nut hunt), soar like a bird, make a pinecone owl — and think about what you do to get ready for winter!

Squirrel Play

Here's a squirrel, with eyes so bright,
> *(form circles around eyes with fingers)*

Hunting for nuts with all its might,
> *(shade eyes with hand and look around)*

Here's its hole, where day by day,
> *(cup one hand to make a "hole")*

Nut after nut it stores away,
> *(poke finger on other hand into the hole)*

When winter comes with the cold and storm,
> *(arms across chest, shivering)*

Squirrel sleeps curled up, all snug and warm.
> *(head on hands, eyes closed)*

How Many Nuts?

Two little squirrels,

(two fingers up)

Scampering through the wood,

(make running fingers)

Two little squirrels,

(two fingers up)

Looking for food,

*(shade eyes with hand
and look around)*

Bushy Tail found one nut,

(hold up one finger on one hand)

Bright Eyes found two more,

(hold up two fingers on the other hand)

How many nuts were there for their winter store?

(count out loud up to the number)

Repeat verses and motions, counting on your fingers:

2. Two nuts ... three nuts ... 1, 2, 3, 4, 5!
3. Three nuts ... four nuts ... 1, 2, 3, 4, 5, 6, 7!
4. Four nuts ... five nuts ... 1, 2, 3, 4, 5, 6, 7, 8, 9!

Go on a nut hunt!

Do you wonder if squirrels "remember" where they hid their nuts in the fall? Ask permission to hide five nuts or buttons around your house. The next day, see if you can find all five. How'd you do at being a squirrel?

The Wide-Eyed Owl

Here's a wide-eyed owl,

> *(form circles around eyes with fingers)*

With a pointed nose,

> *(use finger to extend nose)*

And claws for toes,

> *(curl fingers like claws in front of chest)*

It lives high in a tree,

> *(clasp hands high above head)*

When it looks at you,

> *(form circles around eyes with fingers)*

It flaps its wings,

> *(bend elbows, flap arms)*

And says, "Whoo, whoo-oo-o!"

> *(make owl sounds)*

Make a pinecone owl

What you need: scissors, scraps of felt or paper, marker, glue, pinecone

- CUT OUT EYES, FEET, AND BEAK
- GLUE ON

Little Hands Story Corner™

Owly by Mike Thaler
Good Night, Owl! by Pat Hutchins
Owl Babies by Martin Waddell

Fly with the Birds

Fly high, fly low,

> *(with arms outstretched like wings,*
> *stretch high, then crouch down)*

Fly fast, fly slow,

> *(flap arms very fast, then slowly)*

Let's dive for a drink,

> *(act out diving)*

Let's rest on a hill,

> *(settle arms to side and sit down)*

Fly high, fly low,

> *(stretch arms high and then crouch down)*

Fly fast, fly slow,

> *(flap arms very fast, then slowly)*

Up, up, and away we go!

> *(run with arms out to sides)*

Calling all fall animals!

Play this fall counting game with a partner. Count to three and then say the name of an animal or bird, like an owl. Then imitate the sound of that animal three times — *whoo, whoo, whoo!* Take turns with a friend, naming animals and making their sounds together three times. What a noisy fall forest!

Off to School!

It's a new year at school — hurray! That means new games, more songs, and friends to meet. Ride the "bus," clap and wiggle together, lead others in silly motions as you laugh and play together!

The Wheels on the Bus

To the tune of "The Wheels on the Bus," repeating motion throughout the verses.

The wheels on the bus go round and round,
　　　(turn hands in a circle)
Round and round, round and round,
The wheels on the bus go round and round,
All through the town.

2. The people on the bus go up and down ...
　　　(stand up tall and then crouch down)
3. The doors on the bus go open and shut ...
　　　(hands apart and together)
4. The money on the bus goes *clink, clink, clink* ...
　　　(drop "money" in a slot)
5. The driver on the bus says, "Move on back!"
　　　(thumb over shoulder motion)
6. The wipers on the bus go *swish, swish, swish* ...
　　　(move forearms back and forth like windshield wipers)
7. The horn on the bus goes *beep, beep, beep* ...
　　　(pull or press "horn")
8. The brakes on the bus go *eek, eek, eek* ...
　　　(push foot down as if stepping on brake)
9. The children on the bus go *yak, yak, yak* ...
　　　(fingers to thumb in talking motion)

What other verses can you think of?

✔️ **Check the Calendar**

National School Bus Safety Week

October is early in the school year, so it's a great time to review the bus-riding rules (even if you know them already, a reminder won't hurt!).

- Sit in your seat.
- Wait in line to get on and off the bus. No pushing, please!
- Always wait for the driver to tell you when it's safe to get off the school bus.
- Look up at the driver before crossing in front of the bus. Then, look both ways before crossing a street.
- Never bend down near or under the bus — the driver can't see you!

Way to go (and stay safe)!

Make shape art

Vroom, beep! Make your own bus, truck, or car using shapes of all sizes and colors! Use soup cans, mugs, and small bowls to trace *circles* onto construction paper. Use boxes or paper pads to trace *squares* and *rectangles*.

What you need: shapes (for tracing), pencil, construction paper, child safety scissors, glue

- CUT OUT SHAPES TO MAKE A CAR, TRUCK, OR BUS
- GLUE ON

Everybody Do This!

Try this "follow the leader" action song with a whole group or with another friend. Pat your head and tummy, tickle your elbows, cross your hands and knees, jump or skip in place — whatever motions you think of!

Everybody do this, do this, do this,

> *(act out a motion that everybody else can follow)*

Everybody do this, just like me!

> *(insert the child's name for the "me")*

Everybody do this, do this, do this,

> *(add a second motion to the first one)*

Everybody do this, just like me!

Clap Your Hands

Clap, clap, clap your hands,

> *(slow clapping to the rhythm of the words)*

As s-l-o-w-l-y as you can,

Clap, clap, clap your hands,

> *(fast clapping to the rhythm of*
> *quickly spoken words)*

As quickly as you can.

Repeat verses with new words and motions:

2. Shake, shake, shake your hands ...

3. Roll, roll, roll your hands ...

4. Rub, rub, rub your hands ...

5. Wiggle, wiggle, wiggle your fingers ...

Two Little Hands

Act out these actions as you say them!

Two little hands go clap, clap, clap,
Two little feet go tap, tap, tap,
One little body turns around,
One little body sits quietly down.

I Wiggle

*Wiggle your way through this song
until you're sitting quietly at the end!*

I wiggle my fingers,
I wiggle my toes,
I wiggle my shoulders,
I wiggle my nose,
Now no more wiggles,
Are left in me,
So I will be still,
as still as can be.

Little Hands Story Corner™

The Wheels on the Bus
    by Paul O. Zelinsky
Miss Bindergarten Gets Ready for Kindergarten
    by Joseph Slate
Green Wilma
    by Tedd Arnold
The Awful Aardvarks Go to School
    by Reeve Campbell

Who Helps Us?

Who are the people who help you and keep you safe? Think about the people you see at school, at home, at the store, and delivering or picking up items around town. Yes, lots of people help us every day! Drive a fire truck, direct traffic, hammer away, and make up your own "helping" actions!

Peter Hammers

Peter works with one hammer, one hammer, one hammer,
   (pound one fist)
Peter works with one hammer this fine day.

Repeat verse with added motions:

2. Peter works with two hammers ...
   (pound two fists)
3. Peter works with three hammers ...
   (pound two fists and one foot)
4. Peter works with four hammers ...
   (pound two fists and two feet)
5. Peter works with five hammers ...
   (pound two fists and two feet and nod your head)

 **Check the Calendar**

Labor Day

Labor Day, the first Monday in September, celebrates all those people who take care of others, fix the roads, or do any kind of work. Who works hard at your house? Thank them with a hug, a smile, and a special thank you!

Some People I See

Make up your own actions to act out this rhyme!

Some people bring the milk and eggs,
And fruits and veggies, too,
Some people work in stores and shops,
Selling things to you,
Some people bring the letters,

And then take more mail away,
Some people stop the traffic,
To help me on my way,
Some people move the furniture,
And pack it in a van,
Some people take the garbage,
And empty every can!

I'm a Police Officer

To the tune of "I'm a Little Teapot."

I'm a police officer, with my star,
    (point to "star" on chest)
I help people near and far,
    (point near you, then far away)
If you have a problem, call on me,
    (point to self with thumb)
I'm your friend, as you can see.
    (point to another child)

Traffic Light

To the tune of "Twinkle, Twinkle Little Star."

Twinkle, twinkle traffic light,
  (form circle shape with hands)
Shining on the corner bright,
Stop shines red,
  (hold hand out in "stop" motion)
Go is green,
  (walk in place)
Slow-down yellow's in between,
  (walk slowly to a stop)
Twinkle, twinkle traffic light,
  (form circle shape with hands)
Shining on the corner bright.

Little Hands Story Corner™

Officer Buckle and Gloria
    by Peggy Rathmann
The Jolly Postman or Other People's Letters
    by Janet and Allan Ahlberg
Red, Yellow, Green ... What Do Signs Mean?
    by Joan Holub

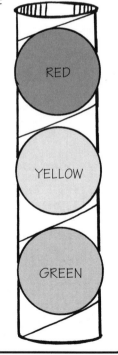

Make a traffic light ...

then play a traffic game!
(*Remember:* red on top, yellow in the middle, and green at the bottom.)

What you need: red, yellow, and green construction paper, paper-towel tube, child safety scissors, glue

- CUT CIRCLES; GLUE TO TUBE

RED

YELLOW

GREEN

The Brave Firefighters

Five brave firefighters sit so still,
(hold up four fingers and thumb)
Until they spot a fire on top of the hill,
(shade eyes with forehead and look around)
Number one rings the bell, *ding-dong!*
(hands clasped high and then low, like a bell)
Number two pulls some black boots on,
(pull hands up legs)
Number three jumps on the fire engine red,
(jump in place)
Number four puts a fire hat on her head,
(hands on head)
Number five drives the red fire truck,
(pretend to drive)
Turn left and right so you don't get stuck!
(sway left and right)
Whoooo! Whooo! Hear the fire truck say,
As all of the cars get out of its way,
(move arms as if pushing something aside)
Whish! Goes the water from the fire hose spout,
(rub palms together)
And quicker than a wink, the fire is out!
(clap hands)

 **Check the Calendar**

Fire Prevention Week

During Fire Prevention Week in October, people change the batteries in their smoke alarms. Where is the smoke alarm in your house? Ask a grown-up to make sure it works. Then, visit your local fire station — you might even get to sit in a real fire truck!

Little Hands Story Corner™

Clifford the Firehouse Dog
by Norman Bridwell
Curious George at the Fire Station
by Margret and H.A. Rey

Celebrate the Season! ◆

In the fall, many families carve pumpkins, dress up in costumes, and eat harvest treats like pumpkin pie and cranberry relish. What's your favorite fall tradition? Act like a Halloween pumpkin, strut and gobble like a Thanksgiving turkey, toast pumpkin seeds, and make witch and wizard hats to celebrate the season!

Halloween Sort

Listen carefully — and then play this game!

If you are a girl and wearing black, wink your eyes.

If you are a boy, jump up high,

If you are a girl, wave hello,

If you are wearing orange, tap your head,

If you are going trick-or-treating, snap your fingers,

If you have raked some leaves, tap your feet,

If you are going to be a witch for Halloween, give a cackle.

☑️ Check the Calendar

It's Halloween!

The last day of October is when all the ghosts and witches come out — the pretend ones, that is! Part of the fun of Halloween is dressing up as something make-believe — a scary witch, a spooky ghost, a silly clown, even Superman! Or you can pretend to be something (or someone) that's real, like a bright orange pumpkin, a famous ballerina, or a baseball player. Whatever you choose to pretend to be, it's still you under your costume!

Did You Ever See a Jack-o'-Lantern?

To the tune of "Did You Ever See a Lassie?"

Did you ever see a jack-o'-lantern,
A jack-o'-lantern, a jack-o'-lantern,
Did you ever see a jack-o'-lantern with
no face at all?
> *(point to face)*

With no eyes,
> *(point to eyes)*

And no nose,
> *(point to nose)*

And no mouth,
> *(point to mouth)*

And no teeth,
> *(point to teeth)*

Did you ever see a jack-o'-lantern
with no face at all?
> *(point to face)*

Have some Halloween fun!

Try this:

- Fly like a bat
- Roll like a pumpkin
- Crawl like a spider
- Prowl like a cat
- Sway like a scarecrow
- Fly like a witch
- Hoot like an owl

Five Little Pumpkins

Five little pumpkins sitting on a gate,

(thumb and four fingers pointing up)

The first one said, "Oh my, it's getting late!"

(fold first finger down)

The second one said, "There are witches in the air!"

(fold second finger down)

The third one said, "But I don't care!"

(fold third finger down)

The fourth one said, "I'm ready for some fun!"

(fold fourth finger down)

The fifth one said, "Let's run and run and run!"

(fold thumb in)

"W-h-o-o-o-o-o" went the wind, and out went the lights,

(clap hands)

And the five little pumpkins rolled out of sight!

(roll hands around each other)

Little Hands Story Corner™

Create a "creepy" reading nook by draping a dark cloth over a big box and reading inside!

Pumpkin, Pumpkin by Jeanne Titherington

There's a Nightmare in My Closet by Mercer Mayer

Where the Wild Things Are by Maurice Sendak

Make tasty toasted pumpkin seeds

What you need: old newspapers, a fresh pumpkin, bowls, spoons, cookie sheet, oil, salt

Scoop the seeds from a cut pumpkin into a large bowl. Separate the seeds from the pumpkin glop by hand (ooey-gooey!). Spread the rinsed seeds on a cookie sheet, drizzle them with oil, and sprinkle with salt. Have a grown-up bake the coated seeds in the oven at 300°F (150°C) until toasted. Yum!

The Witch on Halloween

Join with some friends in this Halloween circle game.
Think up verses until everyone is in the center!

To the tune of "The Farmer in the Dell."

Chorus (sung at the beginning and between each verse)

The witch on Halloween, the witch on Halloween
    (the "witch" stands in the center of the circle
    as others join hands and circle around)
Heigh-ho, let's trick or treat, with the witch on Halloween.

1. The witch chooses a goblin, the witch chooses a goblin,
    (the "witch" chooses another child to go in the center)
    Heigh-ho, let's trick or treat, the witch chooses a goblin.

2. The goblin chooses a bat ...
3. The bat chooses a cat ...
4. The cat chooses an owl ...
5. The owl chooses a spider ...
6. The spider chooses a pumpkin ...
7. The pumpkin chooses a scarecrow ...
8. The scarecrow chooses a ghost ...

Last verse:

They all run and hide, they all run and hide,
Heigh-ho on Halloween, they all run and hide!

Make a witch (or wizard) hat

What you need: black construction paper
(12" x 18"/30 cm x 45 cm), tape, child safety scissors,
stickers or other decorations

• MAKE CONE SHAPE
  TO FIT YOUR HEAD;
  TAPE SIDES
• TRIM BOTTOM
• DECORATE

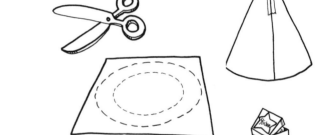

To make a brimmed hat:
Have a grown-up cut
out a large donut-
shaped piece of
cardboard and
tape it to the rim.

The Turkey Strut

To the tune of "The Hokey-Pokey."

You put your right wing in, you put your right wing out,

(right arm to the center of the circle and out again)

You put your right wing in, and you shake it all about.

(right arm to the center of the circle and shake)

You do the turkey strut, and you turn yourself around,

(strut like a turkey, head bobbing around in a circle)

That's what it's all about!

2. You put your left wing in ...

(left arm)

3. You put your drumstick in ...

(leg)

4. You put your stuffing in ...

(tummy)

5. You put your wattle in ...

(head)

6. You put your tail feathers in...

(backside)

7. You put your turkey body in...

(whole self)

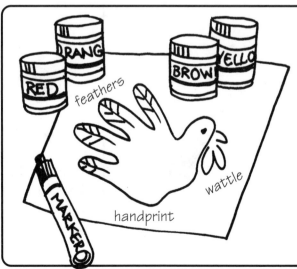

feathers

handprint

wattle

Handprint a turkey

What you need: white paper; brown, orange, yellow, and red tempera paints; black marker

- MAKE A BROWN HANDPRINT
- PRINT A RED WATTLE
- ADD ORANGE AND YELLOW "FEATHERS"

The Turkey

The turkey is a funny bird,
Its head goes wobble, wobble,
(shake head up and down)
But all it says is just one word,
(hold up one finger)
Gobble, gobble, gobble!

 Check the Calendar

Thanksgiving and American Indian Month

Have you heard the story about the Pilgrims, who sailed on the *Mayflower* to America almost 400 years ago? The story is also about the native people of the northeastern woodlands of North America. They taught the Pilgrims how to grow corn and other vegetables, hunt for wild turkeys, dig clams, and harvest wild berries. Without their help, the Pilgrims couldn't have survived!

In the fall, after the harvest, the Pilgrims and the Wampanoag (Wam-pa-NO-ag) Indians celebrated with a feast that lasted three days! It was a special time of friendship.

At Thanksgiving, celebrated in November in the United States and in October in Canada, families and friends gather to give thanks for food, warm homes, and being together. The month of November is also American Indian Month, honoring all the native people who lived in this land long before the Pilgrims arrived.

What special foods do you eat at Thanksgiving? Some of those same foods might have been served when the Pilgrims and Indians feasted together, too!

Pilgrims and Indians

Pilgrims and Indians on three special days,

(hold up three fingers)

Came together in friendship to eat, dance, and play.

(pretend to eat and dance)

The Indians went hunting and brought lots of meat.

(shade eyes with forehead and look around)

The Pilgrims picked berries and cooked many treats.

(pretend to pick berries)

They sat down together and each began to say,

(sit down, head bowed)

That they were very thankful, each in their own way.

Little Hands Story Corner™

Thanksgiving Day
by Gail Gibbons
Cranberry Thanksgiving
by Wende Devlin
Clifford's Thanksgiving Visit
by Norman Bridwell
A Turkey for Thanksgiving
by Eve Bunting

Make easy cranberry relish

What you need: 12 oz (300 g) cranberries, 1 orange (peeled and seeded), $3/4$ to 1 cup (150 to 200 g) sugar

Have a grown-up help you combine cranberries, orange, and sugar in a blender or food processor. Serve the relish at Thanksgiving!

Grandma's Glasses

Here are Grandma's glasses,
> *(form circles around eyes
> with fingers)*

Here is Grandma's hat,
> *(hands on head)*

This is the way she folds her hands,
> *(fold hands)*

And lays them in her lap.
> *(folded hands in lap)*

Here are Grandpa's glasses,
> *(form circles around eyes
> with fingers)*

Here is Grandpa's hat,
> *(hands on head)*

This is the way he folds his arms,
> *(fold arms across chest)*

Just like that!
> *(say with emphasis)*

Make Thanksgiving place cards

Thanksgiving dinner is a time for families to gather together. Maybe you go to your grandparents' house for Thanksgiving, or other special relatives come to visit you. Make place cards and set them at each person's place to welcome all your guests!

What you need: index cards, marker

- FOLD INDEX CARDS IN HALF; WRITE NAME OF FAMILY MEMBER ON EACH ONE
- DECORATE CARDS

WELCOME, WINTER!

Brrr! Feel those cold winds blow! No matter what the weather is like outside, you can have some winter fun inside. Be a snowflake, gently falling through the air, or make a big, round snowman. Find out if Mr. Groundhog spots his shadow! Create a paper candle to welcome the winter solstice, and celebrate the holidays with songs and crafts. Yes, there are lots of wonderful things to do in winter!

The Changing Season

Winter brings chilly days, frost on the windows, glistening icicles, and sparkly snowflakes! Feel those cold winds as you pretend to put on your mittens and hat and play in the snow. Or, warm up to the season with clapping and hopping rhymes!

The North Wind Is A-Blowin'

What happens when the north wind blows?
Act out this rhyme to find out!

Stretch, stretch way up high,
On your tiptoes reach the sky!
Bend way down and touch your toes,
Then stand up and touch your nose,
With arms up high, sway to and fro,
As the north wind blows!

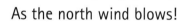

My Little Red Nose

Where did you get that little red nose?
    (point to nose)
Jack Frost kissed it, I suppose,
    (nod yes)
He kissed it once, he kissed it twice,
    (hold one finger up, then two)
Poor little nose, it's as cold as ice!
    (hug self and shiver,
    covering your nose
    from cold)

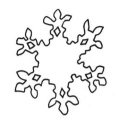

Snowflakes Falling

Snowflakes, snowflakes falling down,
    (hold hands high)
Softly, quietly to the ground,
    (flutter fingers down to floor)
They form a blanket soft and white,
To comfort plants through winter's night,
    (pat floor gently with hands)
See the snowflakes as they play,
    (flutter hands and fingers in air)
Swirling, twirling on their way,
    (twirl around with fluttering hands)
What a pretty, sparkly sight,
When all the earth is dressed in white!
    (clap hands)

**Little Hands
Story Corner™**

*Make an igloo with white sheets for
your story corner!*
The Snowy Day
    by Ezra Jack Keats
White Snow, Bright Snow
    by Alvin Tresselt
The First Snowfall
    by Anne and Harlow Rockwell

Make snowflake ornaments

To hang your snowflake, punch a hole in the top and thread it with ribbon.

What you need: paper, scissors, glitter, glue, hole punch, ribbon

FINISHED:

• DECORATE WITH GLITTER; ADD RIBBON

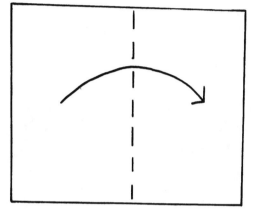

1: FOLD IN HALF

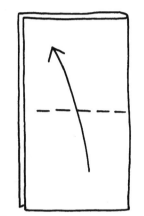

2: FOLD IN HALF AGAIN

3: FOLD AGAIN TO FORM TRIANGLE

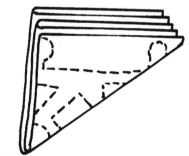

4: CUT OUT A DESIGN

Snow, Snow

To the tune of "Row, Row, Row Your Boat."

Snow, snow, see the snow,
    (hold hands high)
Falling to the ground,
    (flutter fingers down to floor)
Take some snow and pack it tight,
    (pack pretend snow in hands)
And make it nice and round.
    (form circle with hands)

Roll, roll, roll the snow,
    (roll hands)
Roll it on the ground,
    (roll ball of "snow" along the floor)
Stack it tall, don't let it fall,
    (stack a big "snowball")
A snowman in a mound!
    (form circle shape with arms)

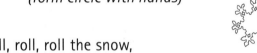

**Little Hands
Story Corner™**

The Snowman by Raymond Briggs
The Biggest, Best Snowman by Margery Cuyler
The Biggest Snowball Ever! by John Rogan
Snowflake Bentley by Jacqueline Briggs Martin

Make a fluffy snowman

What you need: markers, construction paper, cotton balls, glue, precut circles of felt

- DRAW (OR TRACE) THREE CIRCLES FOR THE BODY; GLUE ON COTTON
- GLUE ON FELT BUTTONS, EYES, AND MOUTH
- DRAW HAT AND ARMS

This Is the Way We Get Dressed in Winter

What clothes do you put on as the air outside gets chillier? Act out the motions to the tune of "Here We Go 'Round the Mulberry Bush."

This is the way we get dressed for winter,
Get dressed for winter, get dressed for winter,
This is the way we get dressed for winter,
As the wind blows colder.

Repeat with new actions and words, and add your own verses:

2. This is the way we put on snowpants ...
3. This is the way we put on our boots ...
4. This is the way we put on our coats ...
5. This is the way we put on hats ...
6. This is the way we put on mittens ...
7. This is the way we put on our scarves ...

Last verse:

This is the way we get dressed for winter ...
Now let's go out and play!

Play winter day charades

Use only motions to act out a guessing game of winter activities.

- Make angels in the snow
- Pretend to walk over deep snow
- Roll snowballs
- Fall in the snow and then get up and shake the snow off
- Ice skate on a pond
- Go ice fishing
- Ride a dogsled
- Bring in firewood
- Zoom down a hill on your skis

My Mittens

Mittens for the snow time,
(fingers flutter down like snow)
When the world is white,
Mittens for my two hands,
(hold up two hands)
Mittens left and right,
(wave left hand, then right hand)
Mittens with a thumb place,
(thumbs up)
Mittens warm and snug,
(hug self as if nice and warm)
Mittens make me feel like
A bug inside a rug!
(wrap one hand over the other, like a blanket)

Match your mittens

Hang up your mittens for a winter decoration!

What you need:
construction paper cut in mitten shapes,
markers, hole punch, yarn

• DECORATE MITTENS
• PUNCH HOLES; TIE TOGETHER

Mitten Rhyme

Thumbs in the thumb place,
  (thumbs up)
Fingers all together,
  (fingers up together, thumbs tucked in)
We always put our mittens on,
  (fingers up together, thumbs out to sides)
When it's chilly weather!
  (hug self and shiver)

Little Hands Story Corner™

Mrs. Toggle's Zipper
  by Robin Pulver
The Mitten
  by Jan Brett
Mitten
  by Alvin R. Tresselt
Flannel Kisses
  by Linda Crotta Brennan

Peas Porridge Hot

Peas porridge is an old-fashioned British expression for pea soup. Do you think you'd like to have soup that is "nine days old"?

Peas porridge hot,

> *(slap knees, clap hands together, and then*
> *clap partner's hands with your hands*)*

Peas porridge cold,

> *(repeat action above)*

Peas porridge in the pot,

> *(slap knees, clap hands together, and then*
> *clap partner's right hand with your right hand)*

Nine days old.

> *(slap knees, clap hands together, and then*
> *clap partner's left hand with your left hand)*

Repeat the same motions for the second verse:

Some like it hot,
Some like it cold,
Some like it in the pot,
Nine days old.

*Younger children can just clap to the rhythm.

Popcorn

One little kernel,
> *(hold up one finger)*

Sleeping in the pot,
> *(head on hands, eyes closed)*

Turn on the heat,
> *(turn "switch" with hand)*

And watch it pop.
> *(clap hands)*

Popping, popping popcorn,
> *(jump in place)*

A crunchy, crunchy treat,
> *(stomp on the ground)*

Pour on the butter,
> *(pour with hands)*

And let me eat!
> *(gobble up "popcorn"!)*

Little Hands Story Corner™

Stone Soup retold by Heather Forest
Popcorn by Alex Moran
The Popcorn Dragon by Jane Thayer
The Popcorn Book by Tomie de Paola

Make a popcorn wreath

What you need: precut cardboard in doughnut shape, yarn, popped corn, glue (in a dish)

- GLUE ON YARN LOOP
- DIP POPCORN INTO GLUE AND PRESS IN PLACE
- GLUE ON TINY YARN BOWS

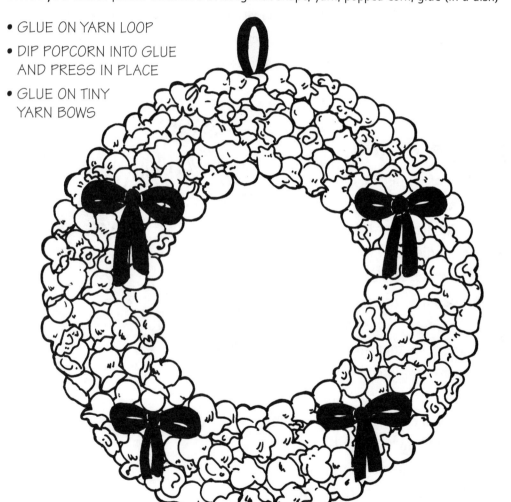

Celebrate the Season!

The holidays are here! It's so exciting! During the winter months, people all over the world with many different beliefs hold festive gatherings. What special things do you do every year to celebrate your family's beliefs and traditions? Make a paper candle, sing and dance a holiday rhyme, and clap your hands as you experience the many different winter traditions!

Candles Bright

In the dark of winter's night,
(head on hands, eyes closed)
We light candles that burn bright,
We light candles that are large,
(arms out to sides)
We light candles that are tall,
(on tiptoes, arms stretching high)
We light candles that are round,
(arms forming a circle)
And we light candles that are small,
(crouch down)
In the dark of winter's night,
(hands under head as if sleeping)
We light candles that burn bright!

Make a flickering candle

To "light" the candle, push the paper flame up through the tube.

What you need: toilet-paper tube, construction paper (white, green, red, yellow), glue, craft or Popsicle stick

- GLUE WHITE PAPER AROUND TUBE
- GLUE ON GREEN HOLLY LEAVES AND RED BERRIES
- GLUE YELLOW FLAME ON STICK

Check the Calendar

The Winter Solstice

In winter, does the sun go to bed before you do? Winter nights come early — it's the darkest and coldest time of the year! The winter solstice (around December 20) is the shortest day and the longest night of the year.

During December, people of many different beliefs use candles or lights as part of their holiday traditions to brighten the darkness of winter. Do you bring an evergreen tree inside and decorate it with sparkly lights or light Christmas candles, a Hanukkah menorah, a Kwanzaa kinara, or other special candles?

Little Hands Story Corner™

Dear Rebecca, Winter Is Here
    by Jean Craighead George
The Winter Solstice
    by Ellen Jackson

Hanukkah Candles

On each of the eight nights of the Jewish holiday of Hanukkah, another candle on the candle holder, called a menorah, *is lit using the center candle, the* shamash. *Count out the little candles on your fingers, holding up another finger with each line.*

One little candle,
Two little candles,
Three little candles in a row,
Four little candles,
Five little candles,
Six little candles all aglow,
Then come seven,
And last comes eight,
Hanukkah is so much fun —
I can't wait!

Welcome, Hanukkah

To the tune of "Twinkle, Twinkle Little Star."

Welcome Hanukkah, feast of lights,
    (hold arms out in front, bring toward chest)
Let's burn a candle every night,
    (arms overhead, waving slightly like a flickering candle)
Watch the dreidel spinning 'round,
    (spin body in a circle)
Eat the latkes, crisp and brown,
    (rub tummy)
Welcome Hanukkah, feast of lights,
    (repeat first motion)
With candles shining for eight nights.
    (hold up eight fingers)

Make a splatter-paint menorah

What you need: precut cardboard menorah shape, blue and yellow construction paper, white tempera paint, old toothbrush, drinking straws, scissors, glue

- PLACE THE MENORAH ON THE BLUE CONSTRUCTION PAPER.
- DIP THE TOOTHBRUSH IN THE WHITE PAINT AND SPLATTER-PAINT AROUND THE MENORAH.
- LET DRY.
- REMOVE THE CARDBOARD MENORAH.
- CUT FOUR STRAWS IN HALF; GLUE ON THE PAINTED MENORAH.
- GLUE ONE LONG STRAW IN THE CENTER.
- CUT YELLOW PAPER FLAMES; GLUE TO THE TOP OF EACH CANDLE.

Little Hands Story Corner™

Latkes and Applesauce:
A Hanukkah Story
    by Fran Manushkin
Potato Pancakes All Around:
A Hanukkah Tale
    by Marilyn Hirsh

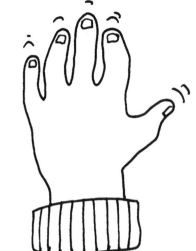

Five Little Candles

Count out the five candles of the Christmas Advent wreath, holding up one more finger with each line.

One little candle shines with all its might,
Two little candles twinkle lovely light,
Three little candles make a pretty sight,
Four little candles glow so strong and bright,
Five little candles flicker in the night,
Warm, glowing candles: a Christmas delight!
("flicker" all five fingers like candles)

I Can Be as Tall as a Christmas Tree!

I can be as tall as a Christmas tree,
(stand up tall on tiptoes, hands stretching high)
As round as Santa,
(hands in front, making a big round belly)
And as tiny as an elf,
(crouch down)
I can bend like a candy cane,
(bend sideways at waist, with head and arms tilted over)
Look like a star,
(spread arms and feet wide)
And prance like a reindeer!
(prance in place, with front "hooves" in the air)

Make a pinecone mobile

Pinecones from evergreen trees create a festive mobile! Attach a string to each end of the mobile and hang it in a sunny window where it will sparkle!

What you need:
pinecones, glue, glitter, string, small branch

- DAB GLUE ON PINECONES AND SPRINKLE WITH GLITTER
- TIE ON BRANCH

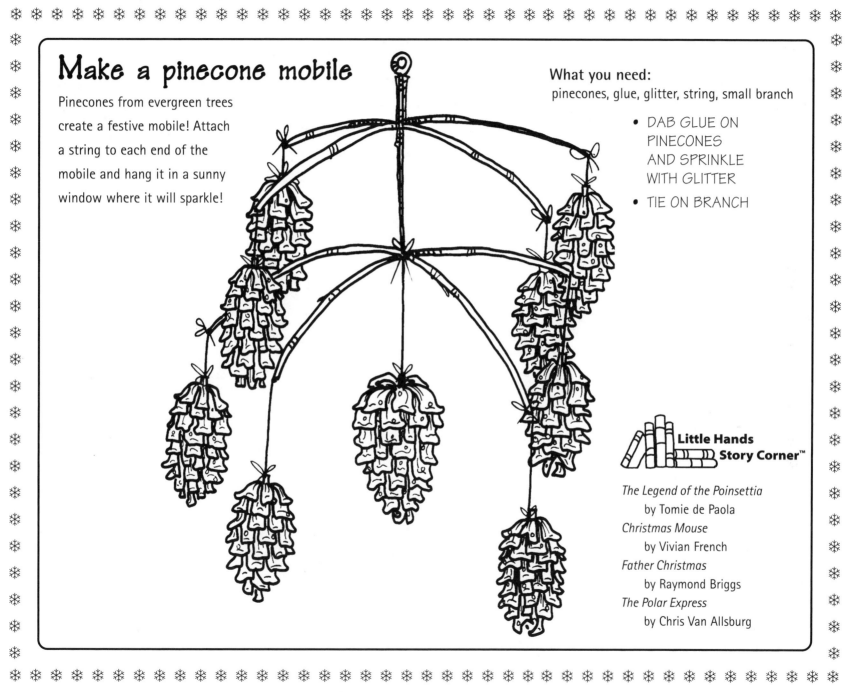

Little Hands Story Corner™

The Legend of the Poinsettia
  by Tomie de Paola
Christmas Mouse
  by Vivian French
Father Christmas
  by Raymond Briggs
The Polar Express
  by Chris Van Allsburg

Kwanzaa Lights

During Kwanzaa (December 26 to January 1) people of African descent celebrate their cultural heritage. The name Kwanzaa, from the Swahili language, means "first fruits" of the harvest. One of the symbols is an ear of corn for each child. It is a time for African Americans to feel proud and joyful as they celebrate family and community. A candle is lit on each of the seven days: the black center candle first, then the three red and three green candles alternately.

Kwanzaa is Here!

To the tune of "Three Blind Mice."

Red, green, black,
> *(one hand out to one side, the other hand out to the other side, then both hands in center to form a "candle")*

Red, green, black,

Kwanzaa is here,
> *(clap hands to the beat)*

Kwanzaa is here,
> *(clap hands to the beat)*

We'll gather with friends and family,
> *(arms out to sides, shoulder height)*

There's special corn for kids like me,
> *(point to self)*

We'll light a candle for unity,
> *(hold "candle" in one hand, "light" with the other)*

Kwanzaa is here!

Little Hands Story Corner™

K is for Kwanzaa: A Kwanzaa Alphabet Book
    by Juwanda G. Ford
Seven Candles for Kwanzaa
    by Andrea Davis Pinkney

Weave a Kwanzaa mat

Make an *mkeka*, or straw mat, to place on the table during Kwanzaa and cover with ears of corn and other Kwanzaa harvest symbols.

What you need: black, red, and green construction paper, child safety scissors, tape

- FOLD BLACK PAPER IN HALF
- CUT SLITS; STOP 2" (5 CM) FROM TOP EDGE

- WEAVE 1' (30 CM) WIDE GREEN AND RED PAPER STRIPS
- TRIM ENDS; TAPE OR GLUE

The New Year Is Here!

To the tune of "Mary Had a Little Lamb,"
following the motions.

Clap your hands with New Year's cheer,
New Year's cheer, New Year's cheer,
Clap your hands with New Year's cheer,
It comes just once a year.

2. Tap your toes ...
3. Snap your fingers ...
4. Hug your arms ...
5. Click your tongue ...
6. Take a bow ...
7. Raise your arms ...
8. Wave to friends ...

 Check the Calendar

Happy New Year!

Hurray! January 1 is the beginning of a whole new year! And guess what? During that year, you'll turn a whole year older, too! Count out how old you will be at your next birthday. Wow!

Have some yarn-and-paint fireworks

Ring in the New Year with a painted fireworks display!

What you need: black or dark blue construction paper, yarn, tempera paints (red, gold, white, green, orange, blue, or other bright colors), old toothbrush

- DRAG YARN THROUGH PAINT, THEN OVER PAPER
- SPATTER WITH TOOTHBRUSH DIPPED IN PAINT

Dr. King, He Had a Dream

To the tune of "B-I-N-G-O."

Dr. King, he had a dream,
> *(hand to forehead, then over head)*

Of peace and harmony,
> *(arms out to the side, then hold hands together in front)*

P-E-A-C-E,
> *(clap hands to the beat)*

P-E-A-C-E,
> *(clap hands to the beat)*

P-E-A-C-E,
> *(clap hands to the beat)*

And every person free.
> *(arms out to sides)*

On his birthday, let us sing
> *(hand to mouth, then in the air)*

Of peace and harmony,
> *(arms out to the side, then hold hands together in front)*

P-E-A-C-E,
> *(clap hands to the beat)*

P-E-A-C-E,
> *(clap hands to the beat)*

P-E-A-C-E,
> *(clap hands to the beat)*

The way our world should be!
> *(make a "world" circle with arms and hands)*

✓ Check the Calendar

Martin Luther King, Jr. Day

On the third Monday in January, we honor the birthday (January 15, 1929) and memory of Dr. Martin Luther King, Jr., and remember his work for peace and equal rights for people of all races. He was a great leader and a wonderful friend to all people!

Make hand-to-hand art

What you need: markers, construction paper (various colors), child safety scissors, glue, poster board

We are all friends

- TRACE HANDS ON PAPER; CUT OUT
- GLUE CIRCLE OF HANDS ONTO POSTER BOARD

Pass the Heart

Pass a cardboard heart around in a circle to the beat and rhythm, and then put it on the floor when the song ends. Sing fast, and then very slowly!

To the tune of "Row, Row, Row Your Boat."

Pass, pass, pass the heart,
Pass it round and round,
Pass, pass, pass the heart,
Now place it on the ground!

 Check the Calendar

Happy Valentine's Day

On February 14, do you like to make valentines to send (and to receive them as well!)? Valentine's Day is a wonderful time to show family and friends how much they mean to you. Your friends might be old or young, boys or girls, sisters or brothers, even your pets. The best thing about friends is that they care about you and like spending time with you!

Five Valentines

Five little valentines were sitting in place,
> *(hold five fingers up)*

The first valentine was covered in lace,
> *(hold up one finger)*

The second valentine said, "I love you,"
> *(hold up two fingers)*

The third valentine said, "I love you, too!"
> *(hold up three fingers)*

The fourth valentine was as happy as could be,
> *(hold up four fingers)*

It knew the fifth valentine was addressed to me!
> *(hold all five fingers up)*

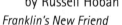
Little Hands Story Corner™

Frog and Toad Are Friends
> by Arnold Lobel

Best Friends for Frances
> by Russell Hoban

Franklin's New Friend
> by Paulette Bourgeois

One Zillion Valentines
> by Frank Modell

The Valentine Bears
> by Eve Bunting

Sign "I love you"!

The language of the deaf, American Sign Language (ASL), uses hand signs and body gestures — some from everyday motions you already know! Can you do these?

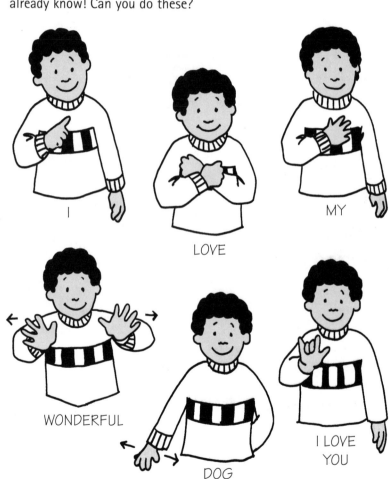

I

LOVE

MY

WONDERFUL

DOG

I LOVE YOU

Where Is Mr. Groundhog?

To the tune of "Ten Little Indians."

Where, oh, where is Mr. Groundhog?
(look around, with hand to forehead)
Where, oh, where is Mr. Groundhog?
Where, oh, where is Mr. Groundhog?
He's sleeping in his burrow.
(head on hands, eyes closed)

Shhh, he's peeking out of his hole ...
(hold index finger to mouth)
Now what will he do?
"Oh, no!"
(say words and hold hands on either side of head)

Mr. Groundhog sees his shadow.
(look behind at your "shadow")
Mr. Groundhog sees his shadow.
Mr. Groundhog sees his shadow.
Six more weeks of winter!
(hold up six fingers)

✓ Check the Calendar

Groundhog Day

Groundhogs, also called woodchucks, have a special day of their own — Groundhog Day! The legend says that if the groundhog sees its shadow on February 2, there will be six more weeks of winter. If it's cloudy, and it doesn't spot its shadow, then winter is supposedly over. Hmmm. What do you think?

Have some shadow day fun

Be a sleepy groundhog. Snuggle in a pretend burrow, wake up after a long sleep, give a big stretch, crawl to the opening of the burrow, and look out. Do you see your shadow?

Big and little shadows. Go outdoors and see your shadow at different times of day, such as in the morning, at noon, and in the afternoon. How are your shadows different?

MORNING

NOON

AFTERNOON

Little Hands Story Corner™

Wake Up, Groundhog!
by Susan Korman
It's Groundhog Day!
by Steven Kroll
Gretchen Groundhog, It's Your Day!
by Abby Levine

My Hat, It Has Three Corners

George Washington wore a three-cornered hat!

My hat,

(touch head on the word "hat")

It has three corners,

(touch each elbow on the word "corner")

Three corners,

(touch each elbow)

Has my hat,

(touch head)

And had it not three corners,

(touch each elbow)

It would not be my hat!

(touch head)

✓ **Check the Calendar**

Presidents' Day

The birthdays of two very important presidents — George Washington and Abraham Lincoln — are in February. George Washington was our first president and helped fight for our country's independence. Abraham Lincoln was the 16th president and is best known for helping to free the slaves.

Abraham Lincoln

Lincoln hoed the growing corn,
(hoeing motion)
And chopped the family's wood,
(chopping motion)
He built a cabin out of logs,
(hammering motion)
And read all the books he could!
(open hands as if holding a book)

Act like Abe Lincoln!

Abraham Lincoln grew up in a log cabin. His family was poor, and he often went barefoot. Young Abe read by candlelight (there was no electricity back then), studied hard to become a lawyer, and then became president! Act out these motions with some friends about Abraham Lincoln's life and have others guess what you are doing, without using words!

- **Walk with a pretend axe over your shoulders**
- **Chop firewood**
- **Split rails for a fence**
- **Build a log cabin**
- **Make a train to go to Washington**
- **March like soldiers in the Civil War**

Little Hands Story Corner™

If You Grew Up With Abe Lincoln by Anne McGovern
George Washington's Breakfast by Jean Fritz

Make a stovepipe hat

Wear a tall stovepipe hat, just like Abraham Lincoln!

What you need: black construction paper, tape, pencil, child safety scissors

- TAPE PAPER INTO CYLINDER
- TRACE AND CUT CIRCLE; TAPE ON TOP
- TRACE AND CUT LARGE CIRCLE; TAPE ON BOTTOM

JUMP INTO SPRING!

Gardens growing, flowers bursting into bloom, birds nesting, and bunnies hopping — spring is the time to shake off winter and explore the great outdoors! Watch your kite soar, splash through puddles, poke some fat pea seeds into the earth, or hop like a bunny. There are so many ways to celebrate that spring is here!

Celebrate the Season!

How does the weather change in spring where you live? In many places, spring weather means windy days and lots of rain showers. The rain brings spring flowers into bloom, and those breezy days are the best for a high-flying kite! Ah, feel that fresh spring air and the warmth of the sun!

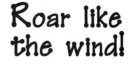

The March Wind

Five little children one March day,
        (hold up five fingers)
Went for a walk just this way,
        (march in place)
The wind blew hard and strong,
        (wave arms above head)
As they walked along,
        (march in place)
It turned them 'round in the street,
        (twirl in place)
Then it blew them off their feet!
        (tumble down)

Roar like the wind!

"March comes in like a lion and goes out like a lamb." That expression describes the winds that sometimes blow in early spring. Can you "roar" like a lion of wind? How would you be a breeze that's as gentle as a lamb?

Let's Fly a Kite!

Pick a windy day,

(wave arms over head)

Pick a kite that's gay,

(make diamond shape with

thumbs and index fingers)

Send it on its way,

(lift hands high as if holding

kite string)

Give it lots of play!

(unwind more string)

Watch it dip and sway,

(dip and sway motion with hand)

Follow it, follow it,

(point to the sky)

Don't let it get away!

(run in place holding kite string in air)

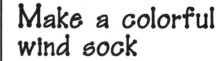

**Little Hands
Story Corner**™

Who Took the Farmer's Hat? by Joan L. Nodset
Curious George Flies a Kite by Margret Rey
Feel the Wind by Arthur Dorros
"Who Has Seen the Wind?" (poem)
by Christina Rossetti

Make a colorful wind sock

What you need: Construction paper, tape, glue, child safety scissors, string, hole punch

- TAPE PAPER TO FORM TUBE
- GLUE CONSTRUCTION-PAPER STREAMERS AROUND BOTTOM
- PUNCH HOLES ON EACH SIDE OF TOP OF TUBE; ATTACH STRING HANGER

Pitter Pat

Pitter pat, pitter pat,

(flutter fingers down to the floor)

Oh, so many hours,

(cross arms on chest)

Though rain may keep me in the house,

(form point of "roof" over head with arms)

It's very good for flowers!

(open arms up into a "blossom")

Check the Calendar

Spring is here!

The first day of spring is usually around March 20. What signs of spring do you see in your neighborhood? In many places, crocuses and daffodils bloom, and you might see the first robins. If you live in a cold climate, early spring might mean melting snow and squishy mud! But wherever you live, the days are getting longer and warmer. Hurray!

Little Hands Story Corner™

My Spring Robin
   by Anne Rockwell
That's What Happens When It's Spring!
   by Elaine W. Good
Over and Over
   by Charlotte Zolotow

Splash!

Rain for the garden,

(flutter fingers down to ground)

Rain for the tree,

(hold arms out like branches)

Rain made the puddle that I didn't see!

(jump forward)

Whoops! Splash!

Little Hands Story Corner™

Henry and Mudge in Puddle Trouble by Cynthia Rylant

What Makes It Rain? by Keith Brandt

Rain by Robert Kalan

Rainy Day Play! by Nancy Fusco Castaldo

Paint with raindrops!

What you need: tempera paint, paper, paintbrush

Paint a few stripes and splotches on your paper. Now, put your painting outside in a gentle rain just for a minute or two. What kind of design did the rain create?

Around the Maypole We Go!

To the tune of "Go In and Out the Window," repeating the motion throughout the verse.

Let's walk around the maypole,
    (walk in a wide circle)
Let's walk around the maypole,
Let's walk around the maypole,
On the first of May.

2. Let's pick a colored streamer ...
    (hold a real or imaginary
    streamer as you walk in a circle)
3. Let's hop around the maypole ...
    (jump in a wide circle)
4. Let's skip around the maypole ...
5. Let's twirl around the maypole ...

 Check the Calendar

May Day

The first day of May is called May Day. In some countries, people have outdoor festivals to celebrate the arrival of spring. They sing and dance around a maypole — a tall pole decorated with flowers and long, colored ribbons.

Make a mini maypole

What you need: cardboard paper-towel tube (wrapping-paper tube is even better!), construction paper, tape, child safety scissors, ribbons

- COVER TUBE WITH PAPER
- TAPE RIBBONS TO TOP

It's Planting Time!

Do you like to dig in the dirt? It's even more fun when you plant a seed or two as well and then watch to see what pops out of the ground! What do the plants in a garden need in order to grow? These songs and rhymes will tell you!

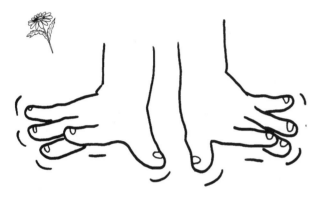

A Little Seed

To the tune of "I'm a Little Teapot."

A little seed I plant in the ground,
    (pat "seed" into "ground")
A little rain comes sprinkling down,
    (wiggle fingers to the ground)
A little sun comes shining through,
    (form circle around head with arms)
I pick a flower just for you!
    (pick "flower" and hold it out in front of you)

Plant a flower basket

What you need: paper cup, potting soil, several flower seeds (marigolds, nasturtiums, and zinnias are colorful and easy to grow), strip of construction paper, stapler

- FILL CUP WITH SOIL
- PLANT SEEDS ABOUT 1" (2.5 CM) DEEP
- STAPLE STRIP TO CUP

Water to moisten and set your cup in a sunny window. Keep the soil damp until the seeds sprout and then water as needed.

Sun power! Turn the cup so your little plant leans away from the window. When you check on it the next day, what do you notice? Your seedling is growing back toward the sunlight! You'll need to keep turning the cup so the plant's stem grows straight and strong.

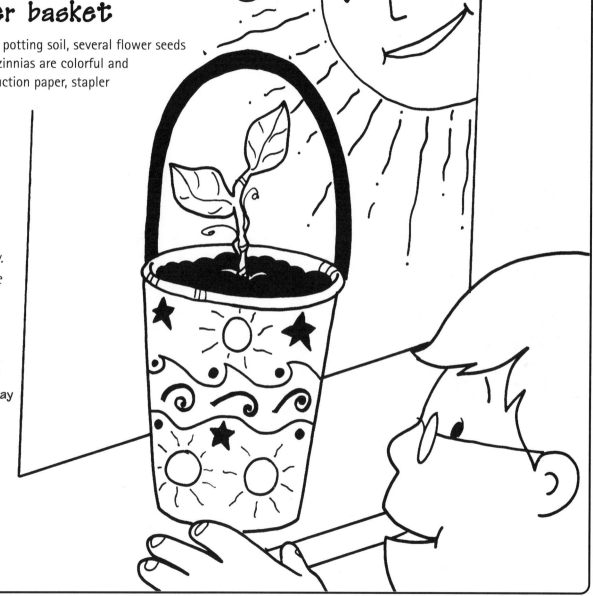

Ten Fat Peas

Ten fat peas in a pea pod pressed,
(make fists with both hands)
One grew, two grew,
(hold up one finger, then two fingers)
And so did all the rest.
(open hands)
They grew and grew and did not stop,
(raise hands over head)
Until one day the pod went pop!
(clap hands overhead)

Peek inside a pea pod

Open a pea pod and look inside. How many peas do you count in there? Did you know that peas are really seeds? That's right, you're eating a mouthful of seeds with every forkful of peas! What are some other seeds that we eat?

Little Hands Story Corner™

The Tiny Seed by Eric Carle
The Reason for a Flower by Ruth Heller
The Carrot Seed by Ruth Krauss

Make a seed-sort mosaic

What you need: a variety of seeds, construction paper, glue

Seeds come in all different shapes, sizes, and colors — how many different ways can you sort yours? Now, glue them on your paper to create different patterns or designs. When you make a picture using small pieces like this, the art you create is called a *mosaic*.

It's Time to Plant the Seeds

To the tune of "The Farmer in the Dell."

It's time to plant the seeds,
>   *(sprinkle "seeds" on the "ground")*

It's time to plant the seeds,
>   *(cover the seeds with "soil")*

Heigh-ho, the derry-o,

It's time to plant the seeds.
>   *(pat the "soil" down)*

The sun shines in the sky,
>   *(make big circle with arms around head)*

The rain begins to fall,
>   *(flutter hands to the ground)*

Heigh-ho, the derry-o,

The seeds begin to grow.
>   *(begin to rise back up)*

And now the plants are tall,
>   *(hold hands above head)*

And now the plants are tall,

Heigh-ho, the derry-o,

There's plenty here for all!
>   *("munch" your harvest)*

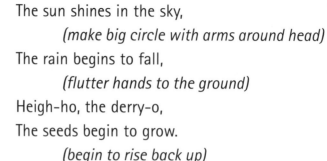

What's under your feet?

On your hands and knees (or lying on your stomach), explore a grassy patch in your backyard or your favorite park. Use a magnifying glass if you like. Do you find other tiny plants growing with the grass? Ants and other bugs at work? There's a lot going on, isn't there?

Make an Earth Day crown

What you need: strip of construction paper, child safety scissors, old magazines or seed catalogs, glue, stapler

- CUT STRIP IN CROWN SHAPE
- CUT OUT PICTURES; GLUE ON
- STAPLE EDGES TO FIT

 Check the Calendar

Earth Day

Planting a garden is a great way to take care of the earth and make it a more beautiful place. Every April 22, people all over the world show they care about keeping the earth clean and healthy by celebrating Earth Day.

There are lots of ways to be a part of Earth Day. You and your family could start recycling if you don't already. Take a walk with your class and pick up any litter you see. Many people leave their cars at home for the day to use less gas and keep the air cleaner. Could you and your family go without your car for a day? Try it and see!

Make popcorn apple blossoms

What you need: blue construction paper, brown and green markers, glue, popped corn

- DRAW A TREE BRANCH AND LEAVES
- GLUE ON POPCORN "BLOSSOMS"

Check the Calendar

National Arbor Day

The last Friday in April is National Arbor Day. Across the United States, we celebrate the importance of planting and caring for trees. If you aren't able to plant a tree in your own yard or community, you can adopt a tree in your neighborhood, at a nearby park, or on your school playground.

Here are some ways to celebrate "your" tree: give it a special name; pick up trash around it; water it often; draw a picture of it; imagine the story of how it grew from a tiny seed and then hold hands with a friend and dance around it, singing "Happy Birthday!"

I'm a Tall, Tall Tree

This is my trunk,
(point to body)
I'm a tall, tall tree,
(hold arms up like branches)
In the springtime, the blossoms,
(make fists)
Cover me,
They open, they open.
(open fingers)

This is my trunk,
(point to body)
I'm a tall, tall tree,
(hold arms up like branches)
In the summer, the breezes,
Blow through me,
(raise arms and wave them back and forth)
I bend, I bend.
(sway back and forth)

This is my trunk,
(point to body)
I'm a tall, tall tree,
(hold arms up like branches)
In the autumn, the apples,
(form circles with thumbs and index fingers)
Form on me,
They drop, they drop.
(clap hands)

This is my trunk,
(point to body)
I'm a tall, tall tree,
(hold arms up like branches)
In the winter, the snowflakes,
(flutter fingers down)
Land on me.
Brrr! Brrr!
(hug self and shiver)

Little Hands Story Corner™

A Tree Is Nice by Janice May Udry
The Giving Tree by Shel Silverstein

Animal Friends

Warm spring weather gets everybody moving — from the birds soaring through the bright, blue sky right down to the worms, deep in the soil. So flap your new baby-bird wings, pop up out of your bunny hole, and wiggle through the gooey mud!

Baby Birds

Up in the sky, the baby birds fly,
(flap arms)
Down in their nest, the baby birds rest,
(cup hands and tuck in thumbs)
With a wing on the left
and a wing on the right,
(fold left arm close to body, then right arm)
Tired baby birds sleep all night.
(head on hands, eyes closed)

Make a high-flying baby bird

What you need: paper plate, scissors (for grown-up use), glue, construction-paper beak, markers

- FOLD PLATE IN HALF; CUT WING FLAPS
- GLUE EDGES TOGETHER
- GLUE ON BEAK; DRAW EYE
- COLOR BIRD

Five Little Birds

Five little birds who have no home,
(hold up five fingers)
Five little trees in a row,
(hold arms straight up over head)
Come build your nests in our branches tall,
(cup hands to form "nest")
We'll rock you to and fro.
(rock the nest back and forth)

Little Hands Story Corner™

Flap Your Wings and *Are You My Mother?*
by P.D. Eastman
Horton Hatches the Egg
by Dr. Seuss

Nesting time!

What you need: bits of soft material like string, cotton balls, dried grass, hay or hair (from your hairbrush or your pet)

Help your feathered friends make their nests as cozy as can be! Put the nesting materials on bushes or tree branches wherever you see lots of birds (near a feeder is perfect). Now, watch the birds carry them off — they'll weave them into their nests!

Little Bunny

There was a little bunny who lived in the wood,

It wiggled its ears as a good bunny should,

> *(hold hands above ears and wiggle fingers)*

It hopped by a squirrel,

> *("hop" along arm with index and*
> *middle fingers)*

It wiggled by a tree,

> *(hold hands above ears and*
> *wiggle fingers)*

It hopped by a duck,

> *("hop" along arm with index and*
> *middle fingers)*

And it wiggled by me.

> *(point to self)*

It stared at the squirrel,

> *(form circles around eyes with fingers)*

It peeked around the tree,

> *(cover face with hands and peek out*
> *between fingers)*

It stared at the duck,

> *(form circles around eyes with fingers)*

But it winked at me!

> *(wink and point to self)*

 **Little Hands Story Corner™**

The Runaway Bunny
  by Margaret Wise Brown
The Tale of Peter Rabbit
  by Beatrix Potter
Tops & Bottoms
  by Janet Stevens

Munch on a "bunny" snack

Bunnies know best — fresh veggies are a healthy, delicious snack! Crunch on some cucumbers and carrots and nibble a fresh lettuce leaf or two!

What Am I?

I have two long ears and a fluffy tail,

(hold hands up next to head for ears,

then hold hand behind you for a tail)

And I like to wiggle my nose,

(twitch nose)

Carrots are my favorite food,

("munch" a "carrot")

And I hop wherever I go!

(hop around)

What am I?

(point to self)

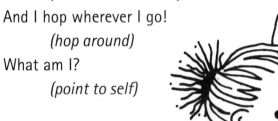

Rabbit, Rabbit, Carrot Eater!

Rabbit, rabbit, carrot eater!

("munch" on index finger)

You know there is nothing sweeter,

(rub your tummy)

Than one carrot every day,

(hold up one finger)

Munch and crunch and hop away!

(jump up and down)

Make soft-as-a-bunny ears

What you need: poster board, scissors (for grown-up use), cotton balls, glue, pink marker, stapler

- CUT OUT EARS; GLUE ON COTTON BALLS
- COLOR CENTERS PINK
- STAPLE STRIP TO FORM CROWN
- STAPLE ON EARS

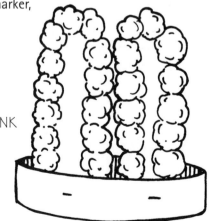

Wiggly Is a Wee Wee Worm

Wiggly is a wee wee worm,
(hold up index finger)
Who wiggles everywhere,
(wiggle finger around)
Can you keep your eyes on it,
As it wiggles here and there?
*(wiggle finger to the left,
then to the right)*

Wiggly starts down at my toes,
(wiggle finger near toes)
And wiggles way up to my nose!
(wiggle finger up to nose)
It wiggles back down without
a peep,
*(wiggle finger down
to waist)*
Creeps into my pocket and
goes to sleep.
*(head on hands,
eyes closed)*

Make a mini worm farm

What you need: patch of earth you can dig in, garden trowel, large jar, water, towel

Fill the jar with soil, then water it. Dig some worms and add them to the jar. Cover it with the towel and set it in a cool place where it won't be disturbed. Does the soil look any different after a day or two?

Be sure to put your worms back in their outdoor home after you've watched them for a while.

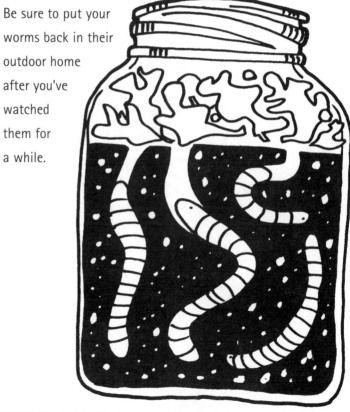

Inchworm, Inchworm

Inchworm, inchworm, you move so slow,
(wiggle forward on tummy)
Inchworm, inchworm, where will you go?
(stop moving)
Inchworm, inchworm, turn to the right,
(wiggle to the right)
Inchworm, inchworm, you'll get there by night,
(put head down and close eyes)
Inchworm, inchworm, turn the other way,
(wiggle to the right)
Inchworm, inchworm, it takes you all day!
(wiggle forward)

Little Hands Story Corner™

Inch by Inch by Leo Lionni
The Big Brag by Dr. Seuss
Wonderful Worms by Linda Glaser

Calling all wigglers!
A real inchworm moves by pushing up its middle section and then sliding its front end forward. Do you move faster when you "inch" along or when you "wiggle" like an earthworm? Have a race with your friends and see!

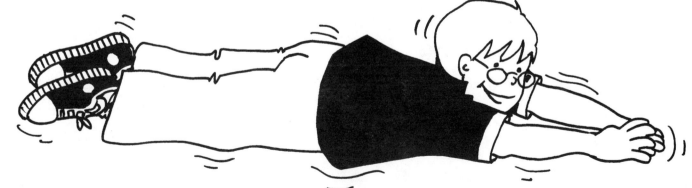

My Pets

Yes, a lot of pets live in my house,
   (nod head and point to self)
I have one gerbil and one white mouse,
   (hold up one finger on each hand)
Two fluffy kittens and two green frogs,
   (hold up two more fingers on each hand)
A goldfish, a bird, and two big dogs,
   (hold up all 10 fingers)
Some people say that's a lot,
Can you tell how many pets I've got?

 **Check the Calendar**

National Pet Week

National Pet Week comes in early May. Most of us already take good care of our pets, but during this week, we are especially kind and loving to our animal friends to let them know how much we appreciate them. If you have a pet, what are some ways to show your pet how special it is? If you don't, ask a neighbor or friend with a pet if you could bring it a special treat.

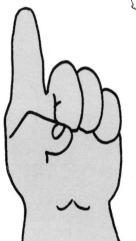

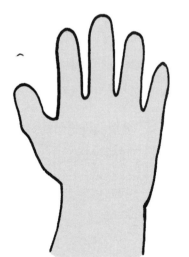

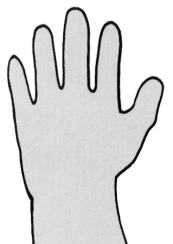

My Kitty

My kitty's tail swishes to and fro,

(bend arm at elbow, wave back and forth)

My kitty sits by a sunny window,

(sit down)

My kitty likes to climb a tree,

(hands "climb" upward)

My kitty's whiskers tickle me!

(wiggle fingers under chin)

Make a curious kitty mask

Wear your mask to prowl around, exploring the sights and sounds of spring!

What you need: Paper plate, scissors (for grown-up use), construction paper, markers, glue, pipe cleaners, Popsicle or craft stick

- CUT OUT EYE HOLES; CUT CONSTRUCTION PAPER EARS
- DRAW FACE; COLOR STRIPES
- GLUE ON WHISKERS AND EARS
- GLUE ON STICK

Five Little Goldfish

One little goldfish lived in a bowl,
(make a bowl shape with hands)
Two little goldfish eat their food whole,
(eating motion with hands)
Three little goldfish swim all around,
(make hands dip and dive in the air)
Although they move, they don't make a sound,
(put finger over lips)
Four little goldfish have swishy tails,
*(hold hands together and swish
them back and forth)*
Five little goldfish have shiny scales.
(hold up five fingers)

**Little Hands
Story Corner™**

Pet Show!
by Ezra Jack Keats
Animal Babies
by Harry McNaught
The First Dog
by Jan Brett
Have You See My Cat?
by Eric Carle

My Turtle

This is my turtle,

(make fist, extend thumb)

It lives in a shell,

(hide thumb in fist)

It really likes its home very well,

(nod head)

It pokes its head out when it wants to eat,

(extend thumb)

And pulls it back in when it wants to sleep.

(hide thumb again)

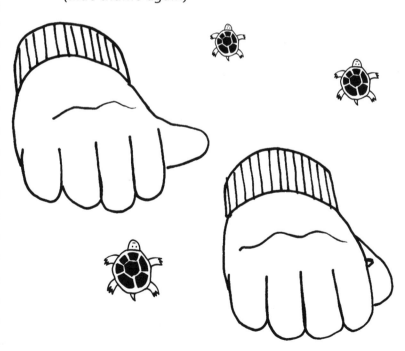

Wear a turtle shell!

What you need: a large paper grocery bag, scissors (for grown-up use), markers

- CUT HOLES FOR YOUR ARMS AND HEAD
- DRAW TURTLE-SHELL PATTERN ON BACK

Slip into your shell and try moving as s-l-o-w-l-y as a turtle! Did you find a sunny spot for a nap? Pull in your arms and head and take a snooze!

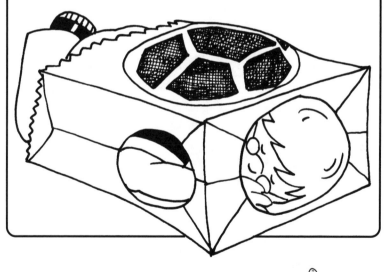

All About Me

New plants poke out of the ground, and baby animals are born and start growing in the spring. And of course, you're growing too! How much bigger are you now than you were a year ago? Are there some favorite warm-weather clothes that don't fit anymore?

Here are some fun ways to stretch and shake that growing body from the tips of your fingers down to all 10 toes!

Just listen to the words of these songs — they'll tell you what motions to do!

Your Little Hands

Take your little hands and go clap, clap, clap,
Take your little hands and go clap, clap, clap,
Take your little hands and go clap, clap, clap,
Clap, clap, clap, with your hands.

2. Take your little toes and go tap, tap, tap ...
   Tap, tap, tap, with your hands.
3. Take your little ears and go wiggle, wiggle, wiggle ...
4. Take your little eyes and go blink, blink, blink ...
5. Take your little arms and go roll, roll, roll ...

Give Your Hands a Clap

Open, shut them, open, shut them,
Give your hands a clap!
Open, shut them, open, shut them,
Put them in your lap,
Creep them, creep them, creep them,
Right up to your chin,
Open wide your little mouth,
But do not let them in!

Handprint a tulip garden

Your hands can make a beautiful spring garden!

What you need: tempera paints in green and bright flower colors, large sheet of paper

- MAKE GREEN STEMS WITH FINGER
- ADD GREEN HANDPRINT LEAVES
- MAKE COLORFUL HANDPRINT BLOSSOMS

On My Head

On my head my hands I place,
On my shoulders, on my face,
On my hips and at my sides,
Then behind me they will hide.
I will hold them up so high,
Make my fingers quickly fly,
Hold them out in front of me,
Now I clap them, 1-2-3!

How tall are you?

Do you have a place on the wall or the back of a door where you mark your height and the date each year? If you don't, ask if you could start one — it's fun to see how much you grow in just one year.

Touch Your Nose

Touch your nose,
Touch your chin,
That's the way this game begins.

Touch your thighs,
Touch your knees,
Now pretend you're going to sneeze.

Touch your hair,
Touch your ears,
Now touch your two lips right here.

Touch your elbows,
Where they bend,
That's the way this touch game ends.

Little Hands Story Corner™

Here Are My Hands by Bill Martin Jr. and John Archambault
Eyes, Nose, Fingers and Toes by Judy Handley
Fun With My 5 Senses by Sarah A. Williamson

Sometimes they work together,

    (hold up hands with fingers together)

Sometimes they work apart,

    (hold up hands with fingers spread apart)

Your fingers can do so many things,

    (wiggle fingers)

Can you think of one to start?

    (show something fingers help you do, like tying your shoes)

Ten Fingers

These are my 10 fingers,

    (hold up both hands)

They do whatever I say.

    (nod head yes)

They help me when I'm eating,

    (bite into an "apple")

They help me when I play.

    (bounce a "ball")

Spell with finger letters!

It's fun to form the letters of the alphabet with your fingers. Try making a curved letter like a C or a straight letter like L (you'll need both hands for some letters). Introduce yourself to a friend by spelling out your name.

Where Is Thumpkin?

Where is Thumpkin? Where is Thumpkin?
(hold up one thumb)
Here I am, here I am.
(hold up the other thumb)
How are you today, sir?
(move one thumb as if "talking" to the other thumb)
Very well, I thank you,
(repeat motion with the other thumb)
Run away, run away.
(hide thumbs behind back)

Repeat verses and motions, using next finger on your hand:

2. Where is pointer?
3. Where is tall man?
4. Where is ring man?
5. Where is pinkie?

The Shape Song

For this song, you'll need a circle, a square, and a triangle cut out of construction paper. Start by sitting down, with your shapes on the ground in front of you — and be ready to change shapes!

To the tune of "Twinkle, Twinkle, Little Star."

Put your circle in the air,
Hold it high and keep it there,
Put your square behind your back,
Now please hold it in your lap,
Put your triangle on your toes,
Now please hold it on your nose.

Hold your circle in your hand,
Now it's time for you to stand,
Wave your triangle at the door,
Now please put it on the floor,
Hold your square and jump, jump, jump,
Now throw your square up, up, up!

**Little Hands
Story Corner**™

Looking Through Shapes at Apples and Grapes by Leo and Diane Dillon
What is Round? and *What is Square?* by Rebecca Kai Datlich
Shapes, Sizes & More Surprises! by Mary Tomczyk

Be a shape detective!

Here's a game you can play indoors or out! From the windows in your room to the signs along the road and the wheels on a car, shapes are all around us. See how many circles, squares, and triangles you can find. What kind of shapes did you find the most of? What's the biggest shape you found? The smallest?

I Looked Inside my Looking Glass

I looked inside my looking glass
*(hold palm like a mirror
in front of face)*
To see what I could see,
I guess I must be happy today,
(smile at mirror)
Because that smiling face is ME!
(point to self)

Little Hands Story Corner™

Today I Feel Silly & *Other Moods That Make My Day*
    by Jamie Lee Curtis
My Many Colored Days
    by Dr. Seuss
What Makes Me Happy?
    by Catherine and Laurence Anholt

Make a "me" collage

What you need: construction paper, child-safety scissors, glue, old magazines

- CUT OUT THE LETTERS OF YOUR NAME; GLUE ON PAPER
- ADD WORDS AND PICTURES THAT TELL ABOUT YOU

SUMMERTIME FUN!

Ah, summer — hot, sunny days when you're outside more than you're indoors! And all around you are adventures to join in! Splash around with your water-loving friends, flutter like a beautiful butterfly and light up a summer night with your firefly "flash," then lead the marching band in a parade! Summer days are the perfect time for just plain silly games, too, like doing the bubble hop or clownin' around to get the giggles going. So celebrate this season of fun in the sun!

Celebrate the Season!

Summer days are extra-long, so you can fill them with extra fun! The sun is high in the sky at this time of year, shining down on all your outdoor adventures! All that sunshine makes lots of cool, shady spots, too, so you can always find the perfect place to play. So let's head outdoors!

Mr. Sun

To the tune of "Mr. Moon."

Oh Mr. Sun, Sun, Mr. Golden Sun,
  (form circle around head with arms)
Please shine down on me,
  (point to self)
Oh Mr. Sun, Sun, Mr. Golden Sun,
  (form circle around head with arms)
Hiding behind a tree,
  (peek out from behind hands)
These little children are asking you,
  (hold hands on both sides of mouth)
To please come out so we can play with you,
  (motion "come here" with hand)
Oh Mr. Sun, Sun, Mr. Golden Sun,
  (form circle around head with arms)
Please shine down on me!
  (point to self)

Make a cheery sun wand

Now you can wave those clouds away!

What you need: tape, construction paper (yellow, red, and orange), paper-towel tube, paper plate, glue

- TAPE YELLOW PAPER AROUND TUBE
- TEAR ORANGE, RED, YELLOW STRIPS; GLUE ONTO PLATE
- GLUE PLATE ON TUBE

 Check the Calendar

The first day of summer

The first day of summer usually comes around June 20. In the Northern Hemisphere, it's the longest day of the year! That side of the earth gets more hours of daylight at this time of year because it's tilted toward the sun. That means you can go back outside to play after supper on a summer night — and it's still light! What else do you love about long, warm summer days?

This Sunny Day

Follow these motions to show how you feel on a bright, sunny summer day!

Who feels happy this sunny day?
If you do, clap your hands and sway.

Who feels happy this sunny day?
If you do, tap your shoulders this way.

Who feels happy this sunny day?
If you do, nod your head and say,
"I'm happy!"

Little Hands Story Corner™

Hot Days
    by Jennifer S. Burke
How Do You Know It's Summer?
    by Allan Fowler
Morning, Noon and Night
    by Jean Craighead George
One Hot Summer Day
    by Nina Crews

Make sun prints

What you need: dark-colored construction paper, flat objects like a key, a coin, a small lid, leaves

Place the objects on the paper and leave it outdoors on a sunny day (keep the leaves in place with small rocks) or in a sunny window. After a few hours, take off the objects. What do you find?

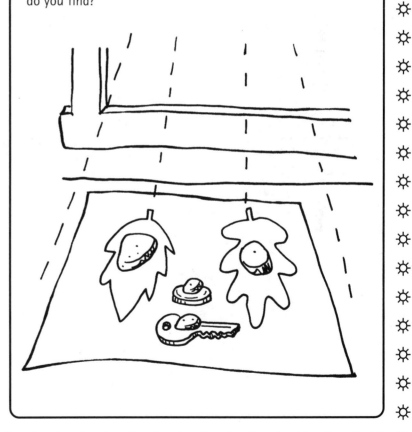

Have a shadow play!

What do you find lots of on a sunny day?
Shadows! They're great for all kinds
of outdoor fun!

- **Play Shadow Tag.** The person
  who is "it" tries to tag another
  player's shadow with her own.
  Then that person becomes "it."
  When all the shadows have
  been tagged, the game is over.

- **Let's cool off!** What do we
  call shadows cast by tall objects
  like houses or tall, leafy trees?
  Shade! After your game of
  Shadow Tag, find a cool,
  shady spot. Feel the difference?

**Little Hands
Story Corner™**

The Shadow Book by Beatrice Shenks de Regniers
Shadows Here, There, and Everywhere by Ron Gour
Bear Shadow by Frank Asch
"I Have a Little Shadow" (poem) by Robert Louis Stevenson

Hear the Thunder

To the tune of "Frère Jacques."

There is thunder, there is thunder,
   (clap your hands)
Hear it roar, hear it roar,
   (cup hands to ears)
Pitter patter raindrops, pitter patter raindrops,
   (flutter fingers down)
I'm all wet! I'm all wet!
   (shake hands)

There is lightning, there is lightning,
   (hold hands up and "flash" fingers)
See it flash, see it flash,
   (form circles around eyes with fingers)
Pitter patter raindrops, pitter patter raindrops,
   (flutter fingers down)
I'm all wet! I'm all wet!
   (shake hands)

Little Hands Story Corner™

Why Does Lightning Strike? by Terry Martin
Big Rain Coming by Katrina Germein
Flash, Crash, Rumble, and Roll by Franklyn M. Branley
Pooh and the Storm that Sparkled by Isabel Gaines

Where's the storm?

The next time you're indoors waiting for a thunderstorm to pass, you can figure out how far away it is! When you see a bolt of lightning, start counting, "One thunderstorm, two thunderstorms," and so on, until you hear the thunder. The number you reach tells you how many miles/km away the storm is. Try it again a few minutes later. Is the storm moving closer or moving away? How does the thunder sound now?

Independence Day

Beat a drum,

("beat" a drum)

March along,

(march in place)

With a great big
"Hip hurray"!

Wave a flag,

*(raise hand and
wave "flag")*

Sing a song,

It's Independence Day!

(clap hands)

See the fireworks,

*(raise arms over head
and open out to sides)*

They are booming,

*(cover ears with
hands)*

High up in the sky,

(point to sky)

Happy Birthday to America,

It's the Fourth of July!

(clap hands)

**Little Hands
Story Corner™**

Hats Off for the Fourth of July!
  by Harriet Ziefert
*Fireworks, Picnics, and Flags:
The Story of the Fourth of
July Symbols*
  by James Cross Giblin
Parade
  by Donald Crews
Where Do Balloons Go?
  by Jamie Lee Curtis

Make a flag to wave!

What you need:
white and blue construction paper,
glue, adhesive stars, red marker,
tape, drinking straw

- GLUE BLUE SQUARE
  ON WHITE PAPER;
  DECORATE WITH STARS
- DRAW RED STRIPES
  ON SQUARE
- TAPE ONTO STRAW

Where's My Balloon?

Once I had a balloon,
(make balloon shape with hands)

That I held tight to me,
(bring shape close to body)

There was a great big POP!
(clap hands)

Now there's no balloon to see!
*(hold palms upward
and shake head)*

✓ **Check the Calendar**

The Fourth of July

Every summer, Americans throw a big party to celebrate the birth of the United States as a country. Many towns celebrate the Fourth of July with parades, barbecues, and fireworks to say "Happy Birthday, America!" And what's a birthday party without balloons?

Draw a big bunch of balloons

Draw a picture of yourself holding the strings of these colorful balloons!

What you need: construction paper (various colors), child safety scissors, glue, string, markers

- CUT OUT BALLOONS; GLUE ON PAPER
- GLUE ON STRINGS

A Bug's Life

Bugs are just about everywhere you look in summer — buzzing around the flowers, crawling on the leaves and through the grass, zooming through the air, even banging on your screen at night.

Bugs Are Neat!

Butterflies fly, and ladybugs, too,
(flap arms)
Ants crawl quickly 'cause they have a
lot to do,
(creep fingers up opposite arm)
Spiders like to spin a web,
(twirl index finger)
To catch a tasty treat,
("gobble" a bug)
I love to look at what bugs do,
*(shade eyes with hand and
look around)*
'Cause I think bugs are neat!
(clap hands on "neat")

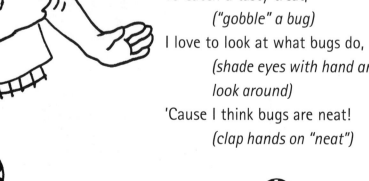

Bug Countdown

Three ants marching in a line,
(march in place, holding up three fingers)
Two big beetles jumping in time,
(jump in place, holding up two fingers)
One caterpillar who just couldn't stay,
(shake head, holding up one finger)
Now there are none because they all went away!
(hold hands out, palms up)

Make a bug hotel

What you need: a glass jar with lots of holes punched in the lid

Search for some interesting-looking bugs to collect in your jar. Be sure to put in some leaves from the plants where you found the insects, along with a little dirt, so they'll feel at home and have something to munch. Sprinkle a few drops of water on one or two of the leaves so they can visit a "bug drinking fountain" when they get thirsty. And after a few days of watching your bugs, be sure to put them back outdoors where they belong.

Little Miss Ladybug

Little Miss Ladybug, sitting on a tree,

(spread out arms like a tree)

She flew down and landed on my knee,

(tap knee)

She asked me if I wanted to play,

(move index finger to show

"come here" and tilt head to side)

But I said "No," so she flew away.

(shake head and flutter fingers away)

Make a paper-plate ladybug

What you need: large paper plate, red and black tempera paints, paintbrush, pipe cleaner, glue

- PAINT PLATE RED
- OUTLINE WINGS IN BLACK
- PAINT BLACK SPOTS AND EYES
- GLUE ON PIPE CLEANER ANTENNAE

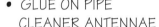

Where Are the Bees?

To the tune of "I'm a Little Teapot."

Here is a beehive,
> *(hold fists together)*

But where are the bees?
> *(shade eyes with hand and look around)*

Hiding away where no one sees,
> *(cover face with hands)*

Watch them all come creeping out of the hive,
> *(open fist and let fingers of other hand creep out)*

One and two and three, four, five!
> *(hold up fingers of one hand, one at a time)*

Busy Bees

Bees gather pollen from the flowers they meet,
> *(hold arms over head, then open out
> into a "blossom")*

And then they make honey for me to eat,
> *(rub tummy)*

Bees are busy flying everywhere,
> *(hold arms out to sides, form circles)*

Buzzing here and buzzing there!
> *("buzz" around like a busy bee!)*

Little Hands Story Corner™

The Very Lazy Ladybug
> by Eric Carle

Bumblebee, Bumblebee, Do You Know Me?
> by Anne Rockwell

Roly-Poly Caterpillar

Roly-poly caterpillar into a corner crept,

(make fingers creep along palm of other hand)

Spun himself a blanket,

(pull "blanket" up to chin)

And for a long time slept,

(rest head on hands with eyes closed)

Roly-poly caterpillar wakened by and by,

(stretch and yawn)

Found himself with pretty wings,

Changed to a butterfly.

*(holding hands together at thumbs,
flutter hands in air)*

Say "Bye-bye, caterpillar! Hello, butterfly!"

A caterpillar changes to a butterfly inside a *crysalis*, a small, hard shell. Curl up tight in a ball with a blanket draped over you, as if you're a sleeping caterpillar. Now, slowly awaken as a beautiful butterfly, let your delicate wings unfold, and flutter away!

Make a clothespin butterfly

This colorful butterfly can land wherever you like!

What you need: square of tissue paper, markers, spring-type wooden clothespin, pipe cleaner

- DECORATE TISSUE PAPER AND BODY
- PINCH TISSUE PAPER WINGS
- ADD PIPE-CLEANER ANTENNAE

Little Hands Story Corner™

The Butterfly Hunt by Yoshi
Where Butterflies Grow by Joanne Ryder
Monarch Magic by Lynn M. Rosenblatt
(for beautiful photos of a caterpillar changing into a butterfly)

Three Little Fireflies

One little firefly, lonely as can be,
(hold up one finger and shake head sadly)
Two little fireflies, blinking in a tree,
*(hold up two fingers on other hand,
then open and close fists next to eyes)*
The first firefly saw the blinking lights,
(form circles around eyes with fingers)
And raced right over with all its might.
(flap arms quickly)

"May I play with you?" said firefly one.
*(hold palms out at sides and tilt
head to one side)*
"Yes," said the others, "until we see the sun."
(nod head)
Now the little fireflies, one, two, and three,
(hold up three fingers, one at a time)
All play together, as happy as can be!
(smile and nod head)

Make a twinkly firefly scene

To see the "fireflies" best, hold
your picture up to the light.

What you need:
black, green,
yellow, and brown
construction paper,
child safety scissors,
glue, hole punch

• GLUE TREE
SHAPES
ON BLACK
PAPER

Back
of paper

• PUNCH HOLES IN BLACK PAPER;
GLUE SCRAPS OF YELLOW PAPER
BEHIND HOLES

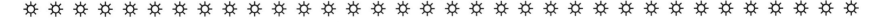

The Eensy Weensy Spider

To the tune of "The Eensy Weensy Spider."

The eensy weensy spider went up the water spout,
(twist hands upward, forming circles with tips of thumbs and forefingers together)

Down came the rain,
(wiggle fingers downward)

and washed the spider out.
(push hands downward)

Out came the sun and dried up all the rain,
(make big circle with arms over head)

and the eensy weensy spider went up the spout again!
(twist hands upward, forming circles with tips of thumbs and forefingers together)

Little Hands Story Corner™

Miss Spider's Tea Party
by David Kirk
Sam and the Firefly
by P. D. Eastman
Life in the Meadow
by Eileen Curra
In the Tall, Tall Grass
by Denis Fleming
The Little Hands Nature Book
by Nancy Fusco Castaldo

Make an up-and-down spider!

What you need: marker, egg-carton section, glue, yarn, scissors, paper-towel tube, hole punch

- DRAW FACE ON CARTON; GLUE ON YARN LEGS
- GLUE YARN TO TOP
- PUNCH HOLE; PULL YARN TO MAKE SPIDER GO UP SPOUT

Make a Splash!

Five Little Fishes

Five little fishes swimming in a pool,
(wiggle five fingers)

The first one said, "Oh my, the pool is cool,"
(wrap arms around body)

The second said, "The pool is deep,"
(hold hand at waist to show depth)

The third one said, "I want to sleep,"
(head on hands, eyes closed)

The fourth one said, "Let's dive and dip,"
(make hands dip and dive in the air)

The fifth one said, "I see a ship,"
(shade eyes with hand)

A boat comes along,
("swimming" motion with hands in front of chest)

And the line goes kersplash,
(clap hands)

And away those five little fishes dash!
(wiggle five fingers away)

Little Hands Story Corner™

Swimmy
  by Leo Lionni
The Rainbow Fish
  by Marcus Pfister
The Little Fish that Got Away
  by Bernadine Cook

I Caught a Fish

1, 2, 3, 4, 5,

(count up on fingers of one hand)

I caught a fish alive,

(catch "fish" in your hands)

6, 7, 8, 9, 10,

(count up on fingers of other hand)

I let it go again.

(open hands to let fish go)

Why did you let it go?

(shrug shoulders)

Because it bit my finger so! Ouch!

(shake finger as if it hurts)

Sponge-paint an ocean of fish

What you need: sponges cut in fish shapes, blue construction paper, tempera paints in shallow dishes, paintbrush

- SPONGE-PAINT DIFFERENT-COLORED FISH
- PAINT SEAWEED, FISH BUBBLES, AND SHELLS

Leap Frog

Crouch down and, with your hands on your ankles,
try leaping like a frog as you say this rhyme.

Leap frog, leap frog,
Easy as can be,
I'll leap with you,
And you leap with me.

Leap frog, leap frog,
On your lily pad,
You can leap farther,
And you're so glad!

Little Hands Story Corner™

Days with Frog and Toad
    by Arnold Lobel
Jump Frog Jump
    by Robert Kalan
Wonders of the Pond
    by Francene Sabin

Hop around — ribbit! ribbit!

You can hop around indoors or out on this lily pond! Or use your pond to play Leap Frog with a friend or two. Have one player squat down on a lily pad and, with your hands on the player's back, leap over her. Can you land on another lily pad? Make frog noises as you play.

What you need: large blue towel or sheet, green construction paper, child safety scissors

• SPREAD OUT TOWEL OR SHEET
• CUT OUT LILY PADS; PLACE IN "POND"

Here Come the Ducks

Here comes the daddy with his great big feet,
(stamp feet)

Here comes the mommy with her feathers so neat,
(pat hair)

Then come the babies all in a row,
(walk with hands waving behind back)

Waddle, waddle, waddle, there they go!
(squat down and wiggle body back and forth)

Be an animal on the go

Can you waddle across the room like a duck? How would you slither like a snake? Fly like an eagle? Gallop like a horse? Now prowl quietly along like a tiger!

Little Hands Story Corner™

Angus and the Ducks
    by Marjorie Flack
The Story About Ping
    by Marjorie Flack
Make Way for Ducklings
    by Robert McCloskey
One Duck Stuck
    by Phyllis Root

Five Little Monkeys

Five little monkeys,

(hold up five fingers)

Swinging in a tree,

(swing arms in front of body)

Teasing Mr. Alligator,

(thumbs in ears, wave fingers)

You can't catch me!

Along comes Mr. Alligator, hungry as can be,

(open and shut arms like alligator jaws)

Snap!

(clap alligator jaws shut)

Repeat verses and motions, counting down on fingers:

2. Four little monkeys ...

3. Three little monkeys ...

4. Two little monkeys ...

Little Hands Story Corner™

Five Little Monkeys Jumping on the Bed and *Five Little Monkeys with Nothing to Do* by Eileen Christelow
Caps for Sale by Esphyr Slobodkina
Curious George by H.A. Rey
Alligator Shoes by Arthur Dorros

Last verse:

One little monkey,

(hold up one finger)

Swinging in the tree,

(swing arms in front of body)

Teasing Mr. Alligator,

(thumbs in ears, wave fingers)

You can't catch me!

Along comes Mr. Alligator, hungry as can be,

(open and shut arms like alligator jaws)

Snap!

(clap alligator's "mouth" shut)

No more monkeys!

Watch out for this hungry alligator!

What you need: green construction paper, markers, cardboard paper-towel tube, tape, scissors (for grown-up use)

- DRAW SCALY PATTERN ON PAPER; TAPE AROUND TUBE

- CUT OUT EYES, LEGS, AND TAIL; TAPE ON

- CUT A V-SHAPED MOUTH

Make the best banana snacks

Hungry little monkeys (and even a hungry alligator!) will gobble up these yummy banana snacks! *Have a grown-up help you:*

- Toss a banana in a blender with strawberries and yogurt for a quick and delicious fruit smoothie.

- Dip a banana in melted chocolate and then freeze it for a sweet treat.

- Fill toothpicks with sliced bananas, blueberries, and chunks of apples, pineapple, and kiwis for delicious fruit kabobs.

Summertime Sillies!

Summer days are feel-good days for fun and giggles with friends, from blowing bubbles to the ultimate in silly summer fun — a trip to the circus!

The Bubble Hop!

To the tune of "Row, Row, Row Your Boat."

Blow, blow, blow, some bubbles,
*(form circles with
thumbs and index fingers)*
Do the bubble hop,
(hop on one foot)
Jump so high,
(jump up and down)
Until they pop,
(clap hands on "pop")
Then you have to stop!
*(hold out hand in
"stop" position)*

Little Hands Story Corner™

Bubble, Bubble
by Mercer Mayer
The Magic Bubble
by Ingrid and Dieter Schubert
Bubble Trouble
by Mary Packard

Bubble Gum, Bubble Gum

Bubble gum, bubble gum, chew and blow,
(form "bubble" with thumb and index finger, hold in front of mouth)

Bubble gum, bubble gum, scrape your toe,
(scrape "gum" off your big toe)

Bubble gum, bubble gum, tastes so sweet,
(rub tummy)

But get that bubble gum off your feet!
(look at the sole of your shoe)

Make bubble art!

Be sure to sign your name to your bubble painting!

What you need: 3 teaspoons dishwashing liquid, $1/2$ cup (125 ml) water and 2 to 3 drops food coloring, a drinking straw, construction paper

Have a grown-up help you mix dishwashing liquid, water, and food coloring in a large bowl. Place the straw in the bowl and blow through it (don't suck in!) until the bubbles rise to the top of the bowl. Place the paper over the bubbles so that it's covered with bubble prints.

The Circus Clown

The circus clown shakes your hand,
(shake hands)

The circus clown plays in the band,
("beat" a drum)

The circus clown has enormous feet,
(stomp feet)

The circus clown loves to eat,
(pat tummy)

The circus clown has a round, red nose,
(point to nose)

The circus clown has white teeth in rows,
(point to teeth)

The circus clown has very sad eyes,
(make a sad face)

He laughs, and frowns, and then he cries,
(laugh, frown, then rub eyes as if crying)

The circus clown bends way down,
(bend down)

What would you do if you were a clown?

Little Hands Story Corner™

Circus by Lois Ehlert
Clifford at the Circus by Norman Bridwell
Circus Family Dog by Andrew Clements
Emeline at the Circus by Marjorie Priceman

Clown around!

What you need: paper plate, hole punch, scissors (for grown-up use), yarn, markers, construction paper, tape

Ask a grown-up to punch holes in the sides of the paper plate and to cut out two eyeholes, too. Knot yarn through the holes. Now you're ready to create a funny clown face to bring on the giggles!

• CUT OUT BIG PAPER SHOES; TAPE ONTO YOUR SHOES

The Elephant

Here comes the elephant, he moves so slow,
(walk slowly in place with big, heavy steps)
He swings his long trunk to and fro,
*(holding hands together, swing arms
back and forth)*
He's so big, he can't even jump,
(shake head as you jump in place)
He sits down with a great,
big thump!
(sit down)

Try it with a trunk

Slip your hand into a sock and try using it as an elephant trunk. What's the smallest object you can pick up? The largest? Imagine eating your supper with your elephant trunk instead of a fork!

Play circus charades

Act out these motions and see if your friends can guess who you are! Remember, no words!

- A great, big elephant
- A goofy circus clown
- A juggler
- A lion tamer
- A tightrope walker
- A trapeze artist

Resources

Holidays/ Commemorative Days

Earth Day
Earth Day Network
811 First Avenue, Suite 454
Seattle, WA 98104
(206) 876-2000
www.earthday.net

Groundhog Day
www.Groundhog.org

Martin Luther King, Jr. Day
usinfo.state.gov/usa/blackhis/
   history.htm

National American Indian/Native
   American Heritage Month
www.education-world.com/
   a_lesson/lesson209.shtml

National Arbor Day
The National Arbor Day
Foundation
100 Arbor Ave.
Nebraska City, NE 68410
(402) 474-5655
www.arborday.com

National Fire Prevention Week
National Fire Prevention
Association
1 Batterymarch Park
P.O. Box 9101
Quincy, MA 02269-9101
www.nfpa.org
www.firepreventionweek.org/
www.sparky.org/

National Pet Week
The American Veterinary
Medical Association
www.avma.org

National Library Sign-Up Month
National Library Week
American Library Association
50 E. Huron
Chicago, IL 60611
www.ala.org

National School Bus Safety Week
National School Bus
Transportation Association
Alexandria, VA
www.schooltrans.com/safeweek

World Food Day
www.fao.org/wfd
www.worldfooddayusa.org

Additional Resources

Storytime Treasures
P.O. Box 2325
Midland, MI
888-38-STORY
www.storytimetreasures.com

National Network for Child Care
www.nncc.org

www.perpetualpreschool.com
www.preschooleducation.com
www.geocities.com/
   ~holidayzone

*Yonder Come Day: Traditional
Music for Children,* by Mary
DesRosiers, 7 Lampman Rd.,
Harrisville, NH 03450.

Index

More Good Books from Williamson Publishing

 Williamson's
Little Hands®
Books ...

SETTING THE STAGE FOR LEARNING

The following *Little Hands®* books for ages 2 to 6 are 128 to 160 pages, fully illustrated, trade paper, 10 x 8, $12.95 US.

Parents' Choice Approved
The Little Hands NATURE BOOK
Earth, Sky, Critters & More
by Nancy Fusco Castaldo

American Bookseller Pick of the Lists
RAINY DAY PLAY!
Explore, Create, Discover, Pretend
by Nancy Fusco Castaldo

Real Life Award
The Little Hands ART BOOK
Exploring Arts & Crafts with 2- to 6-Year-Olds
by Judy Press

ArtStarts
FOR LITTLE HANDS!
Fun Discoveries for 3- to 7-Year-Olds
by Judy Press

Parent's Guide Children's Media Award
ALPHABET ART
With A to Z Animal Art & Fingerplays
by Judy Press

Parents' Choice Approved
The Little Hands BIG FUN CRAFT BOOK
Creative Fun for 2- to 6-Year-Olds
by Judy Press

Early Childhood News Directors' Choice Award
Parents' Choice Approved
2000 American Institute of Physics Science Writing Award
SCIENCE PLAY!
Beginning Discoveries for 2- to 6-Year-Olds
by Jill Frankel Hauser

Early Childhood News Directors' Choice Award
Parents' Choice Approved
SHAPES, SIZES & MORE SURPRISES!
A Little Hands Early Learning Book
by Mary Tomczyk

The Little Hands PLAYTIME! BOOK
50 Activities to Encourage Cooperation & Sharing
by Regina Curtis

Little Hands PAPER PLATE CRAFTS
Creative Art Fun for 3- to 7-Year-Olds
by Laura Check

AROUND-THE-WORLD ART & ACTIVITIES
Visiting the 7 Continents through Craft Fun
by Judy Press

WOW! I'M READING!
Fun Activities to Make Reading Happen
by Jill Frankel Hauser

Parents' Choice Gold Award
FUN WITH MY 5 SENSES
Activities to Build Learning Readiness
by Sarah A. Williamson

MATH PLAY!
80 Ways to Count & Learn
by Diane McGowan & Mark Schrooten

 the original Williamson's
Kids Can!® **Books ...**

The following *Kids Can!®* books for ages 6 to 13 are each 144 to 176 pages, fully illustrated, trade paper, 11 x 8$^1/_2$, $12.95 US.

American Bookseller Pick of the Lists
Oppenheim Toy Portfolio Best Book Award
Parents' Choice Approved
SUMMER FUN!
60 Activities for a Kid-Perfect Summer
by Susan Williamson

Parents' Choice Approved
KIDS CREATE!
Art & Craft Experiences for 3- to 9-Year-Olds
by Laurie Carlson

American Bookseller Pick of the Lists
Oppenheim Toy Portfolio Best Book Award
Skipping Stones Nature & Ecology Honor Award
EcoArt!
Earth-Friendly Art & Craft Experiences for 3- to 9-Year-Olds
by Laurie Carlson

Parents' Choice Recommended
KIDS' ART WORKS!
Creating with Color, Design, Texture & More
by Sandi Henry

Early Childhood News Directors' Choice Award
Real Life Award
VROOM! VROOM!
Making 'dozers, 'copters, trucks & more
by Judy Press

Dr. Toy Best Vacation Product
Parents' Choice Approved
KIDS GARDEN!
The Anytime, Anyplace Guide to Sowing & Growing Fun
by Avery Hart and Paul Mantell

Parents' Choice Gold Award
Benjamin Franklin Best Juvenile Nonfiction Award
KIDS MAKE MUSIC!
Clapping and Tapping from Bach to Rock
by Avery Hart and Paul Mantell

Selection of Book-of-the-Month; Scholastic Book Clubs
KIDS COOK!
Fabulous Food for the Whole Family
by Sarah Williamson & Zachary Williamson

JAZZY JEWELRY
Power Beads, Crystals, Chokers, & Illusion and Tattoo Styles
by Diane Baker

Parents' Choice Gold Award
American Bookseller Pick of the Lists
Oppenheim Toy Portfolio Best Book Award
THE KIDS' MULTICULTURAL ART BOOK
Art & Craft Experiences from Around the World
by Alexandra M. Terzian

Teachers' Choice Award
Parent's Guide Children's Media Award
Dr. Toy Best Vacation Product
CUT-PAPER PLAY!
Dazzling Creations from Construction Paper
by Sandi Henry

Parents' Choice Gold Award
Dr. Toy Best Vacation Product
THE KIDS' NATURE BOOK
365 Indoor/Outdoor Activities and Experiences
by Susan Milord

Parents' Choice Approved
Parent's Guide Children's Media Award
BOREDOM BUSTERS!
The Curious Kids' Activity Book
by Avery Hart and Paul Mantell

TO ORDER BOOKS:

Toll-free phone orders with credit cards:

1-800-234-8791

We accept Visa and MasterCard (please include the number and expiration date).

Or, send a check with your order to:

Williamson Publishing Company
P.O. Box 185
Charlotte, Vermont 05445

E-mail orders with credit cards:
order@williamsonbooks.com
Catalog request: **mail, phone, or e-mail**

Please add $4.00 for postage for one book plus $1.00 for each additional book. Satisfaction is guaranteed or full refund without questions or quibbles.

Prices may be slightly higher when purchased in Canada.

VISIT OUR WEBSITE!

To see what's new at Williamson and learn more about specific books visit our website at:

www.williamsonbooks.com